David O. Oyedepo

WALKING IN DOMINION

WALKING IN DOMINION

Published in Nigeria by:

DOMINION PUBLISHING HOUSE

ISBN: 978-2905-41-0

4th Reprint: June 2008

For further information or permission, write:

DOMINION PUBLISHING HOUSE

Km10, Idiroko Road, Canaan Land, Ota, Nigeria.

Tel: 234-1-7747546, 7747547, 7747548

Or visit: www.davidoyedepoministries.org

E-mail: dph@davidoyedepoministries.org

All Scripture quotations are from the King James Version of the Bible, except otherwise stated.

Contents

Introduction

> ***Say unto God, How terrible art thou in thy works! through the greatness of thy power shall thine enemies submit themselves unto thee.***
>
> Psalm 66:3

We have never seen the kind of power that God is about to display in the Church! The enemies of God will be brought under His footstool; and until this is done, Christ will not come.

The Word of God says, *"Through the greatness of thy power..."*, not through the greatness of thy teachings, sermons, or religious obligations. The Church might have seen power in the past, but God is now talking about the greatness of His power! Christianity without power is a frustrated religion! No matter how religious you are, Pharaoh won't let you go without first a demonstration of God's power; your grammar, education or wealth not withstanding. Paul knew this too well and disclosed the secret of his dominion in 1 Corinthians 2:4:

And my speech and my preaching was not with enticing words of man's wisdom, but in demonstration of the Spirit and of power:

The end-time Church is a Church of power; it is a ruling and reigning Church. This is how the scripture describes it:

And it shall come to pass in the last days, that the mountain of the LORD's house shall be established in the top of the mountains, and shall be exalted above the hills; and all nations shall flow unto it.

Isaiah 2:2

The above scripture is announcing the definite emergence of the exalted Church: the one enthroned with authority by the ways of God. Heaven is out to release the Church into the fullness of her redemptive colour! God will raise men and women of supernatural authority in the Church who will command the attention of nations; they will be men and women of dominion.

The Church will become highly exalted through marvellous insights in the Word of God. It will be Church robed in power, manifesting the many–sided wisdom of God. And I'm here to herald the coming glory of that Church (the coming presence of God – the mighty visitation of God that is coming upon the

Church of Jesus Christ on earth) and to introduce you to the essential force behind its accomplishment.

Friends, we are on the verge of a major event in the body of Christ! God is coming down in the midst of His people such as never was done before! There is a divine programme on; we are moving into the realms of an awakening that the world has never seen before! The Church of Jesus Christ is coming on a power frequency and into realms of beauty, glory, honour, and distinction that will herald His return! We are living in the days of the dominion of the saints of God who are endowed with the supernatural ability to confront oppositions with confidence.

Revelation 5:10 tells us:

> ***And hast made us unto our God kings and priests: and we shall reign on the earth.***

So whether as a priest in the temple, or a king in the palace, in ministry, in business, etc, the ultimate of redemption is to make you reign on the earth. Until you begin to reign in the area where God has placed you, you are not fulfilling your calling. The world should be looking at us to learn how to live! Oh yes! They should be asking us: "Which way?"

Jesus said we (the Church) are a city that is set on a hill (Matt. 5:14). The world should, therefore, be looking up to us; we should command attention. Every redeemed child of God is born to be an attraction. This is made very clear in Deuteronomy 28:1:

> ***And it shall come to pass, if thou shalt hearken diligently unto the voice of the Lord thy God, to observe and to do all his commandments which I command thee this day, that the Lord thy God will set thee on high above all nations of the earth.***

God has destined us to be above only, because we are the righteous seed of the Righteous God. The world should be reading our biographies to locate how to run their system. We are in a time where we should be causing undeniable waves wherever we are, commanding the attention of kings and thrones! This is the time for the Church to take the stage, as we are in the Church age now! See what the Bible says about the Church:

> ***A day of darkness and of gloominess, a day of clouds and of thick darkness, as the morning spread upon the mountains: a great people and a strong; there hath not been ever the like, neither shall be any more after it, even to the years of many generations.***
>
> Joel 2:2

This is talking about the emergence of an army of God right from the midst of gloominess and darkness!

An army designed to enjoy strange affluence, inexplicable abundance, and command strange wealth! The Garden of Eden will be recreated for them. However, outside their camp will be great sufferings and afflictions. This great army will be made up of men and women of unquestionable dominion; an army to be envied, not just by people, but by nations as well! Nations will identify and respect them (Isa. 62:2-4). They shall be modern day Elijahs, who would decide the destinies of nations (1 Kgs. 17:1).

One unique thing about this army is that the blackness around is what will make their distinction remarkable. Jesus said, *"Ye are the light of the world"* (Matt. 5:14). That makes you a pacesetter. People will be tracing your steps to know how to be great. Jesus also said, *"Ye are the salt of the earth"* (Matt. 5:13). That means you are created to matter in your generation. The purpose of salt is to give taste and preserve from decadence. That means this generation needs you to sweeten people's lives, to preserve them from decadence.

All these are pointers to the fact that you are no more an ordinary creature when you become born again. In John 14:12, Jesus makes us understand that we shall do greater works than He did:

Verily, verily, I say unto you, He that believeth on

me, the works that I do shall he do also; and greater works than these shall he do; because I go unto my Father.

Jesus said, you are to do greater works than He did. That means you belong to a higher place than where you are now. You are not born to live the ordinary life. You are created to live a life of marvels. Everybody should be spying on you. You are born for dignity; you are born for prominence. You are born for exploits; therefore, you must not disappoint creation, nor redemption!

Friends, we have to be awake on the inside, in order to matter on the outside. We are in the days of the fullness of the inheritance of the saints. It is, therefore, time to catch what it takes to be in this great move we are in. It's time to understand and embrace the forces that make for your distinction and dominion on the earth. That is what this book is all about. I want to introduce you to some dimensions of the ministry of the Holy Spirit, as it pertains to bringing the saints to the fulfillment of God's prophecies concerning the end-time Church. This is because you need the Holy Ghost to make a difference in your world.

The Church of Jesus is undertaking her final strike against the forces of mediocrity in the Church. The former rain is nothing to be compared with the latter rain. No matter what we saw in the Acts of the Apostles, we haven't seen anything yet! Those were mere forerunners of what God is set to do with the latter day saints. We are now in the actual generation that the world is waiting for. We're in the royal age of the Church; a time where we will be calculating sickness out of our lives, and failure out of our way. We will shine on all fronts in spite of the devil. Instead, the devil would suffer at our hands through the application of the many-sided wisdom of God at our disposal!

So, welcome to the world of dominion!

The Day Of His Power

The Lord said unto my Lord, Sit thou at my right hand, until I make thine enemies thy footstool.

The Lord shall send the rod of thy strength out of Zion: rule thou in the midst of thine enemies.

Thy people shall be willing in the day of thy power, in the beauties of holiness from the womb of the morning: thou hast the dew of thy youth.

Psalm 110:1-3

In God's agenda, there is a day called "The day of

His power." It is the day when the Church will reign and rule in the midst of her enemies. It is a time of dominion, when mortal men will walk like spirits. Redeemed men and women will become spiritual squad missiles on every street, devastating the enemy's camp.

The whole earth is waiting for the manifestation of the sons of God. And God has an agenda to make His people take charge of the entire earth. That day is here! It is not coming; it has come! The agenda of the day of God's power will be in place before Jesus comes. In the day of God's power, His people will be in charge of affairs, resulting in their supernatural lifting.

The kingdom of God is not a kingdom of theology, but a kingdom of power (1 Cor. 4:20). Christianity will no longer be mistaken for religion, as there will be clear manifestations of the supernatural in the Church. It is the power era of the Church, and we are out to show the world that we've got the answer!

God's enemies are already surrendering their arms, because the day of His power has come!

> ***Say unto God, How terrible art thou in thy works! through the greatness of thy power shall thine enemies submit themselves unto thee.***
>
> Psalm 66:3

There is a display of power going on right now. Momentum has been gathering from far and near, and it is about to explode! The Church is taking her rightful position, and Christianity is now very attractive. Everyone identified with it has become enviable personalities. God's people will no longer be ashamed of the gospel, as the highest honour will be to be a Christian. May your place not be lost in the day of His power!

God is fully set for an outpouring of His power upon His Church. This will hasten the coming of the Lord Jesus, as He will remain seated until His Church has taken full charge. I am persuaded that until the power of God begins to explode in us, we will not be ready to welcome the King back home. I am fully persuaded that native doctors will completely run out of business in my days. Witchcraft will become a thing of shame, and the Ogboni cult will begin to stink!

Saints of God who have accepted the responsibility of pressing on are already entering into God's power at various levels, as God no longer deals with the crowd, but with individuals. Luke 16:16 tells us that:

The law and the prophets were until John: since that time the kingdom of God is preached, and every man presseth into it.

The gates are now open, so every man must begin to press. You have a duty to press into your portion. Know for a certainty that Christianity has no taste without power.

Things Are Already Happening!

> ***But upon mount Zion shall be deliverance, and there shall be holiness; and the house of Jacob shall possess their possessions.***
>
> Obadiah 1:17

When you see things happening on their own accord, then you must know that we are in the days of power. It is very clear that we are already in the day of God's power, as testimonies abound that point to this fact.

I attended a meeting where there was a man with only one testis. But as soon as this man stepped into the hall, the missing testis was restored! Also one day at our Kaduna church, an Air Force officer who had brought his friend to church decided to stay and see what was going on. The Holy Ghost got hold of him, and by the time he came back to his senses, he was speaking in tongues! The unique thing is that this gentleman was a staunch muslim! He again burst out in tongues when he got home, and before his wife knew what was happening, she too joined him in speaking in tongues! This is what the day of God's power is all about.

In yet another service, there was a man with a withered hand from an accident at work. While the service was on, an invisible guest walked up to him, grabbed his hand, and there and then, the withered hand was straightened out! There was also the case of a woman who had fire burn scars all over her. In the course of the service, somebody walked up to her and said, "Embrace me." As she rose to embrace this mysterious guest, all the scars vanished!

We are no longer looking for the day of God's power; it has come! We are in the days of His power, the season of the dominion of the Church. It is therefore time to take charge!

How shall we rule in the midst of our enemies? It is through the greatness of His power at work in us. Darkness has no respect for position, status or possessions. Your enemies will not submit because you wear good dresses, but because the greatness of His power is manifested through you. So, it is time to believe God for a release of His power in your life.

Paul the apostle said in 1 Thessalonians 1:5:

> ***For our gospel came not unto you in word only, but also in power, and in the Holy Ghost, and in much assurance...***

We're already seeing this in our days. Jesus said in Mark 16:17:

And these signs shall follow them that believe; In my name shall they cast out devils; they shall speak with new tongues.

A Bible school student from our Owerri campus arrived home to discover that his uncle had just died. The first thing he said was, "Can I see him?" He went in and saw the man, whose nostrils had already been stuffed with cotton wool. He immediately sent all the mourners out of the room, then anointed the dead man, but there was no response. Next, he struck him with his mantle (prayer cloth) seven times, saying, "The God of Bishop David Oyedepo shall bring you back to life." And the dead man jerked back to life!

We have heard several other testimonies of the manifestations of the reality of God's power in the Church, including the dead that were brought back to life. Here are some of them:

"He...Came Back To Life!"

"On getting home from the Communion service last Thursday, my mother told me to drive her to her friend's house, whose husband had just died, and I took my anointing oil along with me. The dead man's first daughter had just arrived from Abuja, and immediately fainted on seeing her mother. Her mother also fainted.

Several people, including my mum, immediately untied their wrappers, and began using it to fan the two of them. I told my mother that there was no need for all that, that we should hand over everything to Christ. But my mother replied, 'This your Christ, when will you finish from it?' I was not very strong in the faith, but I believed God would do everything and perfect it.

Something then ministered to me to bring out my bottle of anointing oil. I obeyed, and poured a little into the lid of the bottle and poured it into the woman's nose. Immediately I did that, she began to scream, 'Pepper, Pepper.' I told her it was no pepper, but the anointing oil, the power of God. I did the same thing to her daughter, who also responded in the same way.

When she got up, she said, 'But what will we do to daddy?' I said, 'Where is daddy?' Her mother told us that the man had suffered from cancer, asthma, and diabetes, and that the doctor said he was dead. I said,

'He is not dead; he's only sleeping. That's what we were told in church.' On getting to the hospital, we met a muslim doctor, who said, 'I'm fasting. Go wherever you want to go. If you want to go there and wake him up, go and wake him up. We've packed him for you.' I said, 'You've not packed anybody, he's only sleeping!'

I went in to the dead man and said, 'There shall be no loss in the mighty name of Jesus.' Both the dead man's daughter and wife started crying again. So, I sent his wife out of the room. My mother said to me, 'Tosin, you've started again.' And I replied, 'Yes, I've started again. God is in control now.' The man's daughter and I began to pray. After about 10 minutes of prayer, the Holy Spirit told me to pour some of the anointing oil on my palm and rub the man's whole body with it.

I did as I was instructed, and we continued praying. In my heart I kept asking the Holy Spirit for what next to do, and I was again instructed to apply some anointing oil on my palm and place it on the dead man's nose. I obeyed, and less than ten minutes later, he sneezed thrice, and came back to life! Right now, the muslim doctor is here in church, to give his life to Christ!"

Okeowo, T.

Dead Woman Now Lives!

"My neighbour shouted throughout the night last week. When my driver came to take the bus for work at five o'clock in the morning, my neighbours gripped him, and asked that he should take a woman to the hospital. My driver came back to tell me that a corpse had been put in my bus, that they wanted him to take it to the hospital.

I went out immediately and saw the woman in the bus, I said, 'I'm a child of God. My bus should not carry a dead body.' So, I ran back into the house and took my bottle of anointing oil and mantle. I told them to open her mouth, and I poured almost the whole content of the bottle into her month, and she swallowed it. I also anointed her eyes. I tied the mantle around her neck, and she immediately took a deep breath. I then told God to revive her. She immediately opened her eyes, and asked for her husband. I told my driver not to bother to take them to the hospital anymore, and I prayed for her. Here is the woman today."

Eke, J.

The saviours are rising already! From now on, when you step into a city, every force of darkness must shiver and bow to you. Why? Because we are in the day of God's power! Salvation has now become cheap, and many are trooping into the kingdom of God because people have seen the futility of following the devil and all his dirty, evil works. It is now time to say to failure, "Go!" and it goes; and to abundance, "Come!" and it comes. It takes power to do this.

The world will respect you, if you will come on this frequency of power. The world has not seen the days we are in before, as God has loaded it with amazing wonders! In these days we are in, as time goes on, we will stop hearing anything about the devil in the Church, because God is pouring out His power into the Church, giving her what it takes to rule in the midst of her enemies. That's dominion!

David said something very interesting in Psalm 63:1-2:

> ***O God, thou art my God; early will I seek thee; my soul thirsteth for thee, my flesh longeth for thee in a dry and thirsty land, where no water is;***
>
> ***To see thy power and thy glory, so as I have seen thee in the sanctuary.***

Nobody sees God's power without first craving for it. We have been blindfolded by religion, which has deceived us into waiting for the day God will do something. But, 2,000 years ago Jesus declared, "It is finished!" So, tell the Lord to show you His right hand now. His hand and arm will provoke favour on your behalf and bring you into liberty and dominion.

Power is a prerequisite for walking in dominion. That is why the Bible in several verses talks about either our receiving power or being given power.

But ye shall receive power...

Acts 1:8

Behold, I give unto you power...

Luke 10:19

But as many as received him, to them gave he power...

John 1:12

But what do we really need power for?

For Release

At the end of every seven years thou shalt make a release...

...It is called the Lord's release.

Deuteronomy 15:1-2

Biblically, the seventh year is the year of release; but there can be no release without power. Power is the instrument for release. When it was time for Moses to embark on a release mission to Egypt, power was the only instrument he needed.

> ***And Moses answered and said, But, behold, they will not believe me, nor hearken unto my voice: for they will say, The LORD hath not appeared unto thee.***
>
> ***And the LORD said unto him, What is that in thine hand? And he said, A rod.***
>
> ***And he said, Cast it on the ground. And he cast it on the ground, and it became a serpent; and Moses fled from before it.***
>
> ***And the LORD said unto Moses, Put forth thine hand, and take it by the tail. And he put forth his hand, and caught it, and it became a rod in his hand:***
>
> Exodus 4:1-4

Until power is on display, release will not come. God Himself knows this. Look what He said to Moses:

> ***And I am sure that the king of Egypt will not let you go, no, not by a mighty hand.***
>
> ***And I will stretch out my hand, and smite Egypt with all my wonders which I will do in the midst***

thereof: and after that he will let you go.

Exodus 3:19-20

The instrument of release placed in Moses' hand was power. It is time to secure this instrument, if walking in dominion is your goal. Every devil will clear off once it is in your hand.

On one cool Easter evening in 1977, a friend and I were sitting down together on the grass, and having a nice time with the Lord, when one good-looking young man walked towards us. But as he got to where we were, he screamed, "What have I got to do with you? Have you come to destroy us before the time?" And he immediately fled into the bush. We never said a word to him, as we were deep in the spirit. Obviously, the evil force in him couldn't pass by without noticing that there was a higher force around.

I have repeatedly declared, "The witch that will look at me in the face is not yet born! The occult man that will ever dare me is not alive anywhere!" Why?

But truly I am full of power by the spirit of the Lord...

Micah 3:8

I know this to be true in my life, as no one who is merely guessing will shout it the way I do.

And thou shalt take this rod in thine hand, wherewith thou shalt do signs.

Exodus 4:17

Power is the principal requirement for total release. The time for your release and freedom has come, and no devil can do anything about it.

For Manifestation

The Church needs the power God is pouring out in order to manifest her sonship.

For the earnest expectation of the creature waiteth for the manifestation of the sons of God.

Because the creature itself also shall be delivered from the bondage of corruption into the glorious liberty of the children of God.

Romans 8:19,21

Your destiny is insecure without the hand of God upon it or God's power at work in you. Even Jesus could do nothing without God's power at work in His life.

How God anointed Jesus of Nazareth with the Holy Ghost and with power: who went about doing good, and healing all that were oppressed of the devil; for God was with him.

Acts 10:38

Even Jesus the Messiah could only do good because God's power was at work in His life. When Moses went in his own might to fight for Israel, he became a fugitive (Ex. 2:11-15). Every mission not backed-up by power ends up in frustration. Only power can make you enter into the realms of manifestation of your sonship. See the kind of power that has been given to you:

> ***Behold, I give unto you power to tread on serpents and scorpions, and over all the power of the enemy: and nothing shall by any means hurt you.***
>
> Luke 10:19

This is power for manifestation, power for dominion! This kind of power is above every other form of power. A sister put it to work, and was delivered from death and destruction. Here is her testimony:

"On the day the Bishop was laying hands on us, when he was to lay hands on me, I wiped his face with my mantle and then wiped my face with it. After Sunday service, I went to visit an in-law at Ijegun, who was ill. I didn't know the bus stop to alight, but I was sure I would find the place.

When I alighted from the bus, I saw a 'To-let' and

'Daycare' sign, and immediately remembered that one of my younger ones needed a house. I then decided to go and find out about the house. A man took me round the house, and told me how much the rooms were going for. I had a shock-like feeling on my body, like an electric shock when he touched me. He then pointed to a place, telling me that that was where the caretaker I had to see was.

But immediately I entered the room he pointed to, the door snapped shut! When I looked around the four-corners of the room, I saw holes dug and filled with blood. I also saw statues, a basin, knives, and all sorts of killing implements. I wondered at what I was seeing.

One of the four men dressed in shorts, and ready to kill, said to me, 'Do you know where you are?' I said, 'I don't know where I am.' He said, 'You won't see the world again. This is your last.' I said, 'This is not the end for me. I'm a child of Jesus.' The man said, 'What nonsense is this woman saying? I don't think you know where you are?' I said, 'I know where I am. The power of God is with me. I'm a child of Jesus. The death I would have died, Jesus died in my stead already.'

I was with my two daughters; one strapped on my back, and the other holding on to my hand. The door was firmly shut behind us, and the killers couldn't come close to us, neither could we go close to them. We all stood at the same spot. I began to shout, 'The blood of Jesus, the blood of Jesus.' The baby on my back joined me in shouting, 'Amen,' and my other daughter was shouting, 'Jesus! Jesus!'

Later, I said, 'The God of our father, David Oyedepo, I'm in difficulty now. If indeed You revealed Your power to Bishop Oyedepo, reveal the same power to me now.' As soon as I said that, I remembered that the Bishop had said we should always carry our bottle of anointing oil. I brought it out from my bag, along with my mantle (the same one I had wiped the Bishop's face with). I poured some of the anointing oil on my palm, anointed my head and the children's heads with it, and poured some on the door and in the room. My daughter shouted, 'Holy Ghost fire!' and immediately fire began to burn in front of us, and smoke filled the whole place!

The people couldn't come to us, and we also

couldn't go to them. The leader of the group said, 'What strange beings are these that you brought? These ones can't be used. Open the door for them to go out.' But the man to open the door said he couldn't come near us to open the door, because of the burning fire. I then began to wave the mantle in the air and threw the remaining oil, along with the bottle, at the door. My daughter again screamed, 'Holy Ghost fire!' and the door opened, we went out of the room!"

— Adegoke, F

That is manifestation of power; the kind the world is waiting for the Church to manifest! Occult forces will lose their market when the sons of God enter their true realm; the world of darkness will become very cheap to handle.

The whole of creation is waiting for the manifestation of the sons of God, and the hour has come for the sons of men to be converted from serving idols to serving the Living God, as the sons of God take their positions of dominion here on earth.

That you and I need God's power to enjoy dominion here on earth cannot be denied. But how can we take delivery of it? What must be in place for us to walk in dominion in the day of God's power? That is what I will be discussing in subsequent chapters.

Chapter 2

Superiority Consciousness

At the end of an eighteen-hour long vision twenty-five years ago, May 1-2,1981, to be precise, the Lord said to me:

"The hour has come to liberate the world from all oppressions of the devil through the preaching of the Word of faith; and I am sending you to undertake this task."

Since the Lord delivered this liberation commission to me, I have seen the kingdom of darkness suffer untold devastations and humiliations, as I went about accomplishing this assignment. I have been sent to humiliate and frustrate the government of Satan here on earth. Along with this commission of liberation came the tools for accomplishing the task.

What I am going to share with you in this chapter is very vital to your walking in dominion. You need to know who you are in Christ: that you are superior, if you are born again. Not only that, you also need to be conscious of your superiority over the devil and all his evils, and to walk in the consciousness of this truth. This is the only way you can be victorious in life. Until you render Satan powerless, you cannot walk in dominion, which will lead to your possessing your possessions.

In Mark 3:27, Jesus tells us why Satan must first be rendered powerless before we can walk in dominion:

> ***No man can enter into a strong man's house, and spoil his goods, except he will first bind the strong man; and then he will spoil his house.***

The first step to triumph in any conflict with the forces of darkness is to see the weakness of the opposition. If you must walk in dominion over the forces of evil, your principal requirement is light. You must see and know that you are superior to the opposition, because God has placed you above. You are seated with Christ Jesus in heavenly places, far above principalities and powers (Eph. 2:6)! You need to know this truth, and walk in its consciousness as well.

No man can enter into his inheritance except he first renders the opposition powerless. Light or knowledge is the way to do this. As long as you have a grasshopper mentality, you will keep hopping about in life. But a superiority mentality (acquired through knowledge) will cause you to live a fulfilled and glorious life in spite of the devil. I have discovered so much of Satan's weakness, that he is no longer a concern to me.

One truth that should also give you a superiority mentality is this one in Revelation 12:10:

> ***And I heard a loud voice saying in heaven, Now is come salvation, and strength, and the kingdom of our God, and the power of his Christ: for the accuser of our brethren is cast down, which accused them before our God day and night.***
>
> Revelation 12:10

The devil is cast down, whereas you are seated high above with Christ! That should give you a superiority mentality! By the efficacy of Jesus' death on the cross at Calvary and His resurrection three days later, there is nothing more left in Satan. By the authority of scriptures and the integrity of the Word of God, the death and resurrection of Jesus marked the final end of the devil's reign here on earth. You must know this, and allow this truth sink into your mentality.

If this truth of scripture can penetrate into your heart, it will illuminate you; and henceforth, anywhere you stand, the forces of hell will know that you know what you are doing. This is how to walk in dominion.

Until you render Satan helpless, you cannot possess your possessions. So many things are being done to celebrate Satan in the Church of Jesus. But I'm glad to let you know that the voice is now sounding to tell you he is worthless! His throne has been destroyed, and he has no more legal hold on your destiny.

Friend, know that there's no power but of God! Anything called power outside God is fake. See what the Bible, which is the final authority, says:

> ***Let every soul be subject unto the higher powers. For there is no power but of God...***
>
> Romans 13:1

> ***God hath spoken once; twice have I heard; this that power belongeth unto God.***
>
> Psalm 62:11

Jesus said in **Matthew 28:18-19**:

> ***...All power is given unto me in heaven and in earth.***
>
> ***Go ye therefore and teach all nations...***

Jesus is saying here, "Let the world know that absolute power is reserved in Me. Let them know I am the only holder of power in heaven and on earth." There is, therefore, nothing called power left in the hands of the devil and all his agents and agencies put together. If all powers belong to Jesus, then what power does the devil have left?

Power changed hands when Jesus rose from the dead. Ever since, all power in heaven and earth was handed over to Jesus. Look what He said on this matter:

> ***I am he that liveth, and was dead; and, behold, I am alive for evermore, Amen; and have the keys of hell and of death.***
>
> Revelation 1:18

If the keys of hell and death are with Jesus, then there is no more power left in the devil. All he has, and which is his trademark, is tricks. But the light of the gospel will always expose him.

The story doesn't end there though. The conclusion of the matter is: Jesus has all power, and has handed it over to the Church (Matt. 28:18-19)! So you are the one God has placed in charge here! Devils are not permitted to be out on the streets, because they have been reserved in everlasting chains, until the great day of judgment (Jude 6). Show them where they belong, and send them back there. Satan has no right and power to harass you any longer, because you are in charge now. So arise, and walk in dominion!

You Must Be Born Again

Only those who are born again can walk in dominion, because the power Jesus received from God is given only to those who are born of God. The Bible says in John 1:12:

> ***But as many as received him, to them gave he power to become the sons of God, even to them that believe on his name.***

Another translation of John 1:12 says God gave them power to manifest as sons of God. Until you receive Jesus as the Son of God, you don't have access to God's power. Salvation makes you a child of power and dominion. Power is the foundation for your new life in Christ Jesus.

The new birth is an initiation into the realm of power. Just as people are initiated into a cult, the new birth initiates you into another world - the world of power. You are initiated into the realm of covenant power on the day you receive Jesus as your Lord and Saviour. Natural life gives way to eternal life, and everything about you becomes new! Your citizenship changes, as you are no more earthly, but heavenly. You are guarded and surrounded by heavenly immunities, as you walk on earthly places.

You need to know this truth, as many don't seem to know it. Ignorance of this truth is why they're suffering the things they're suffering. Salvation is not an escape route to heaven, but a seal of dominion on the earth.

Jesus said to us in Acts 1:8:

> ***But ye shall receive power, after that the Holy Ghost is come upon you: and ye shall be witnesses unto me both in Jerusalem, and in all Judea, and in Samaria, and unto the uttermost part of the earth.***

Colossians 1:13 tells us that God has translated us from the kingdom of darkness into the kingdom of His own dear Son, Jesus. Something is fired into you at new birth that changes your status.

Romans 11:29 says the gifts and calling of God are without repentance. So, whether you know that God gave you power at salvation or not doesn't change the fact that He did. However, though the power is there, until you discover it, you cannot enjoy it. Though every member of the army of Israel was a covenant child, only David knew that he was in a covenant with God. As a result, only he could challenge Goliath and defeat him (1 Sam. 17). All those men in the army of Israel were probably armed with sophisticated weapons, but they had no insight about their covenant position. David, on the other hand, came with just a sling and five smooth stones, but his understanding gave him his position of dominion.

The Bible tells us that Christ is the power and the wisdom of God (1 Cor. 1:24). So, if Christ dwells in you, then the power of God is resident inside you as well. This is a covenant position that guarantees triumph.

Once you are saved, you become a power-loaded personality! Salvation takes you from the realm of weakness into the realm of power. No wonder the Bible says:

> ***And hath raised us up together, and made us sit together in heavenly places in Christ Jesus.***
>
> Ephesians 2:6

To sit together here refers to enthronement. New birth confers on you power to ascend the throne.

And what is the exceeding greatness of his power

to us-ward who believe, according to the working of his mighty power.

Ephesians 1:19

Something is inside you; and I pray that you not only see it, but also enjoy it. It's time to see that you are seated far above, not near below. This is what Christianity is all about. You entered God's kingdom with a power gift package. Many don't know the level of power redemption confers on them, and that is why the Psalmist lamented in Psalm 82:5-7:

They know not, neither will they understand; they walk on in darkness: all the foundations of the earth are out of course.

I have said, Ye are gods; and all of you are children of the most High.

But ye shall die like men, and fall like one of the princes.

Now that you are born again, you are seated far above all powers, names and dominion. You are far above whatever carries a name. You are above spells, enchantments and poison too.

Surely there is no enchantment against Jacob, neither is there any divination against Israel...

Numbers 23:23

If you do not have this insight, you will be like David's elder brothers. But it is time to bring down every Goliath that is harassing your family, business, position, etc. It is time to rise up in dominion, stop sitting down and allowing the enemy to harass you. Instead, you go and harass him!

New birth is not fun; it is no religion. Rather, it represents a change of status, placing you far above all principalities, power and dominion. If you're saved, then you're a power-loaded personality. The new birth connects you by covenant to the original source of power. It is a privileged position, a position of dominion.

The Word Source

The Word of God is the authentic source of power. And we know of course that when you have power, then you have dominion.

> ***It is the spirit that quickeneth; the flesh profiteth nothing: the words that I speak unto you, they are spirit, and they are life.***
>
> John 6:63

God's Word is His Spirit in written form, which when absorbed into your spirit, brings you in contact with power. The Word of God carries enough power to give you dominion in all spheres of life. For example, in the Word is the power to heal.

He sent his word, and healed them, and delivered them from their destructions.

Psalm 107:20

And it came to pass on a certain day, as he was teaching, that there were Pharisees and doctors of the law sitting by, which were come out of every town of Galilee, and Judea, and Jerusalem: and the power of the Lord was present to heal them.

Luke 5:17

The knowledge and understanding of God's Word will cause you to walk in dominion all the days of your life. It is like a hammer, and can break every hardship in your life into pieces.

Is not my word like as a fire? saith the Lord; and like a hammer that breaketh the rock in pieces?

Jeremiah 23:29

A very good illustration of the power in the Word is seen in John 1:1:

In the beginning was the Word, and the Word was with God, and the Word was God.

If the Word is God, it therefore goes without saying that the Word is omnipotent, just as God is All-powerful and undefeatable. The Word then became light, which shone in darkness, and darkness could not handle it! No wonder Paul could boldly declare in Romans 1:16:

> ***For I am not ashamed of the gospel of Christ: for it is the power of God unto salvation to every one that believeth; to the Jew first, and also to the Greek.***

The gospel (the Word of God) carries power, which causes you to walk in dominion. Many years ago, Satan attempted to make himself noticed, by recounting to me all the evils he had wrought in my extended family. For example, sometime ago a relation of mine was electrocuted after leaning on the bathroom wall. But as Satan was playing mind games with me, the quickening power of God on my inside was suddenly stirred up, and I heard a voice say, "There is no power but of God." As the Spirit of God flooded my soul, I became dangerously rude to the devil. I said to him, "Shut up, I'm in charge here! There is no power but of God." The Word gave me dominion over that situation.

Nothing is more authentic than what comes directly from the source. If when anointed men speak something enters into you, how much more when the Most High speaks! Many have encountered power through the spoken Word in diverse forms – through the T.V., audio and video tapes, anointed books, etc.

God's power that causes one to walk in dominion

is present in His Word, so go for it.

Access to the Word

> ***And he said unto them, Unto you it is given to know the mystery of the kingdom of God: but unto them that are without, all these things are done in parables:***
>
> Mark 4:11

Salvation is your primary access into the mysteries contained in the Word of God. Until you're born again the Word of God is like merely reading stories; you just hear it, but do not understand it. Remember the story of the Ethiopian eunuch in Acts 8? He was reading Isaiah 53, but couldn't understand a thing from it, until Philip came on the scene.

Revelation is impossible without salvation. Until you are saved you don't have access to the mysteries of the kingdom of God. And inside these mysteries lie your triumph and dominion. Every scripture carries power; and all you need do is to gain access into them. When once you do, they become your inheritance forever.

A heart for the Word is another way to encounter the mysteries and power contained in the Word of God. The cares of this world and the deceitfulness of riches contend for attention with the Word of God in one's life, such that what one reads at times goes no further than the wayside. The birds of the air come along and eat them up immediately. That is why you need a heart that is fully set for an encounter to get anything from the Word of God.

My strongest source of strength is the Bible. Every encounter I have had in life can be traced to what dropped into my spirit from the Bible. Be always set for an encounter in the Word whenever you read the Bible. It is your access to dominion.

The blood of Jesus is another access to the Word. It is what opens the Book (Bible) for you.

> ***And I wept much, because no man was found worthy to open and to read the book, neither to look thereon.***
>
> ***And one of the elders saith unto me, Weep not: behold, the Lion of the tribe of Juda, the Root of David, hath prevailed to open the book, and to loose the seven seals thereof.***
>
> Revelation 5:4-5

Until the Book is opened, weeping continues! But the Lamb that was slain (Jesus) opened the Book with His blood. Revelation flows ceaselessly when you approach the Book with His blood; that is, by pleading the blood of Jesus.

And after the second veil, the tabernacle which is called the Holiest of all...

Now when these things were thus ordained, the priests went always into the first tabernacle, accomplishing the service of God.

But into the second went the high priest alone once every year, not without blood, which he offered for himself, and for the errors of the people;

Hebrews 9:3, 5-7

Only the high priest went into the holiest of all, once every year, but not without blood (indicating that the way to the inner room of God was not yet open). But after this came the supreme High Priest — Jesus Christ, the Son of God. With His blood He provided a way in for us all forever.

Without the blood you cannot gain access to the holiest of all, where the ark that contains the rod of Aaron that budded and the golden pot with manna are. The holiest of all is the place to go if you desire a good understanding of the covenant. There are some revelations one receives that can only be likened to one actually eating food! No wonder Jesus told His disciples in John 4:32, that He had food to eat that they didn't know anything about. Once you gain access into the holiest of all, you will never scratch to eat again. This is because manna in the golden pot represents unending supplies.

You have remained in the outer court long enough; it's now time to enter the holiest of all, so you can enjoy dominion in life. End-time battles will be fought by the operation of the manifold wisdom of God. We, therefore, need to gain access into the holiest of all, in order to be part of this glorious army.

Now look at your Bible and tell yourself that you will gain access into the mysteries therein. Command the seals around it to be removed, because unto you it is given to know the mysteries of the kingdom of God. Friend, it's time for you and I to walk continuously in power and dominion!

Chapter 4

The Prayer Connection

The heart-felt and sincere prayer of a believer connects him to dominion. David was a man who walked in dominion, and he tells us his secret:

> ***O God, thou art my God; early will I seek thee: my soul thirsteth for thee, my flesh longeth for thee in a dry and thirsty land, where no water is;***
>
> ***To see thy power and thy glory, so as I have seen thee in the sanctuary.***
>
> ***Because thy lovingkindness is better than life, my lips shall praise thee.***
>
> Psalm 63:1-3

David desired to see God's power and glory, so he sought God early in prayers. Jeremiah 29:13 gives us an assurance of what happens when we seek Him:

> ***And ye shall seek me, and find me, when ye shall search for me with all your heart.***

You need to seek for God's power with the whole of your heart, in order to walk in dominion. David said, *"My soul thirsteth for thee and my flesh longeth for thee..."* This is a desire that comes from within.

Elijah was another man that walked in dominion, and his secret was prayer – heart-felt prayer. Power was released every time he prayed. James 5:17 tells us the kind of prayer he prayed:

> ***Elias was a man subject to like passions as we are, and he prayed earnestly that it might not rain: and it rained not on the earth by the space of three years and six months.***

It is time to tune in to this frequency, because it takes heart–communication with God for you to encounter power that results in dominion. Note that Elijah prayed earnestly, not loudly. This is how the Amplified Bible renders James 5:16: *"The earnest (heartfelt, continued) prayer of a righteous man"* which *"makes tremendous power available"* and is *"dynamic in its working."*

Power is released when you talk to God from your heart. So many people make so much noise while praying, but their heart is not in it. The woman with the issue of blood said in her heart, *"If I may but touch but his clothes, I shall be whole"* (Mk. 5:28). And she encountered power when she did. It was a silent, but sincere desire or prayer from the depth of her heart; and she came out victorious and on top, as she was instantly delivered from a 12-year affliction.

Ask yourself, "What is my heart craving for?" God will only answer what comes from within. The day Hannah went to Shiloh, the high priest did not understand what she was doing, but thought she was drunk. Hannah then said to him, *"I am a woman of a sorrowful heart, who is pouring her heart out to God"* (I Sam. 1:15). This is what touches heaven; and it is the only way to connect with the power from on high, which culminates in dominion.

When the son of the widow of Zarephath died, all Elijah said was, *"O Lord my God, I pray thee, let this child's soul come into him again"* (1 Kg. 17:18-21). This was a heart-to-heaven communication. You too can get connected now, and your heavens will open and you will walk in dominion. The time has come for God to hear your voice. Ask Him to cause you to see the reality of His power as recorded in His Word.

We need the power of God today. It is the answer to all the harassments of the devil (Lk. 10:19). Dominion responds to effectual fervent prayers, the kind Elijah prayed on Mount Carmel. This will tame the devil, and make every lion around you look like a dog.

You don't enjoy dominion by merely wishing it; you get it by praying. Not modern day prayer, but divinely approved, sincere, heart-felt ones. The kind you stay on at until the answer comes.

Dominion doesn't just drop on you. Every one that walks in dominion today went all-out for it. I went up to a mountain to pray many years ago, and the first thing that welcomed me when I got there was a viper that landed from a tree. I said to myself, "Lord I thank You, for this is an indication that this is Your garden, because the serpent was present in the garden of Eden." After that, rain came, and there was no shelter to hide out there on the mountaintop. The sun came next, and again I was right under its scorching heat. All because I was in search of power that will cause me to live a life of dominion. At the end of the third day when I was released to go home, the Lord said to me, "Henceforth, I have touched your tongue with a coal of fire. Whatever you declare from now on, you will see it." That was the day my tongue was anointed for dominion!

You are a priest and a king, meant to reign on the earth. God did not mark you out to be a prayer project. You were created to present the petitions of others to God, not to become a matter of concern to others, one to be constantly presented to God. You must react to your situation in heart-felt prayers.

The gift of power will not come until you stir it up. There's a power deposit already inside you, but it takes prayer to cause it to be released. Prayer is the stirring instrument that causes the release of power. This was why Jesus always separated Himself a great while before dawn, to seek the face of His Father. He was busy stirring up the gift of God in Him. Friend, until you begin to seek God's face in prayer, you won't have access to manifestations and dominion.

Many are, however, loaded, but cannot see the deposits of that virtue in them. They are still sick, battered, beaten and frustrated, while the answer they need is right inside them. Until Zion travails, she will not bring forth (Isa. 66:7-8). If you don't want to travail in prayers, then you won't enjoy dominion here on earth.

After the Lord called me into ministry, I spent the

following twenty-six months in praying and seeking His face. I prayed warfare kind of prayers, tearing down and building up. I'm glad to let you know that till date, I've never needed to borrow, nor lacked what to eat!

When you begin to respond in prayer to every challenge that comes your way in life, then you are on your way to the top. Jesus prayed all night long in order to select His twelve disciples. Businessmen, you need more insight than paperwork, and this will come through the help of the Holy Spirit as you stand in prayers.

A time came when the apostles were downcast; they had been beaten and assaulted. So they went back to their own company to report. As they reported the matter, their immediate response was prayer, not discussion. What happened thereafter put them back in their place of dominion.

> ***And when they had prayed, the place was shaken where they were assembled together; and they were all filled with the Holy Ghost, and they spake the word of God with boldness.***
>
> ***And with great power gave the apostles witness of the resurrection of the Lord Jesus: and great grace was upon them all.***
>
> Acts 4:31,33

Friend, it is time to pray the same kind of earth-shaking prayer they prayed.

Please note that prayer is a spiritual adventure, and we need the help of the Holy Spirit to excel in it. You cannot excel in prayer through the energy of the flesh. We need reinforcements that will help put down the flesh, so we can engage in effectual and fervent prayers. Romans 8:26 says:

> ***Likewise the Spirit also helpeth our infirmities: for we know not what we should pray for as we ought: but the Spirit itself maketh intercession for us with groanings which cannot be uttered.***

The Holy Spirit is the force that helps our weaknesses, so we can effectively engage in prayer. Receive that Spirit right now, in Jesus name! It is the Spirit that quickens your mortal body to approach God in sincerity and truth. I release the Spirit of grace and supplication upon you right now! It will carry you along, until your answers come.

The Church has been sent to help the world. The entire world is waiting for us. This is why God is revealing to us now the things we need to know to accomplish this task. God has not given you the spirit of fear, but the spirit of power, love, and of a sound mind (2 Tim. 1:7). Receive the grace to stir up that gift right now!

Instruments Of Dominion

God has provided the Church with some very powerful covenant instruments for enforcing her dominion here on earth. But note that whereas He has provided the arms, it is our responsibility to know how to use them and actually use them, and not be like the children of Ephraim, who though armed turned and fled from the battle (Ps. 78:9). We must know how to use our God-given implements; otherwise our dominion here on earth will only be wishful thinking.

I will identify and discuss how to use some of these

instruments in this chapter.

The Name Of Jesus

The name of Jesus is a power tool for walking in dominion. It is an unbeatable force in the conflicts of life. The name of Jesus reigns wherever the sun shines, and at the mention of it, every knee bows – whether of things on the earth, things underneath the earth, and things in heaven. No wonder the Bible describes it as a strong tower.

> ***The name of the Lord is a strong tower: the righteous runneth into it, and is safe.***
>
> Proverbs 18:10

The name of Jesus is a strong tower, an institution of power. Once you invoke that name in faith, a strong tower is erected round about you. Peter called upon that name at the gate Beautiful, and his dominion over sickness was established. Hear what he said, and what happened afterwards:

> ***Silver and gold have I none; but such as I have give I thee: In the name of Jesus Christ of Nazareth rise up and walk.***
>
> Acts 3:6

There was an explosion of power at the mention of the name of Jesus, such that a man that was crippled from birth rose up and began to leap and jump! When all the people saw the lame man healed, they gathered around him, Peter and John. And when Peter saw this, he said to them:

> ***...Ye men of Israel, why marvel ye at this? or why look ye so earnestly on us, as though by our own power or holiness we had made this man to walk?***
>
> ***The God of Abraham, and of Isaac, and of Jacob, the God of our fathers, hath glorified his son Jesus; whom ye delivered up and denied him in the presence of Pilate, when he was determined to let him go...***
>
> ***And his name, through faith in his name, hath made this man strong, whom ye see and know: yea, the faith which is by him hath given him this perfect soundness in the presence of you all.***
>
> Acts 3:12-16

The name of Jesus gets things done. It is not just a title; but a possession. That is why Peter said, "Such as I have." You need to possess the name.

The name of Jesus has inbuilt power, that allows anyone who possesses and uses it to walk in dominion. It is a gift to the Church, for our reign here on earth. Jesus said:

> ***And these signs shall follow them that believe; In***

> ***my name shall they cast out devils; they shall speak with new tongues;***
>
> ***They shall take up serpents; and if they drink any deadly thing, it shall not hurt them; they shall lay hands on the sick, and they shall recover.***
>
> Mark 16:17-18

That is dominion! The name of Jesus is a reservoir of signs and wonders. It unleashes signs and wonders when invoked in faith. Anointing goes forth when the name of Jesus is invoked in faith, just like when you spray a room with insecticide. The name is poison to every work of the devil. The wicked just has to bow to the power it carries. And the good news is that all who believe have the right to use that name, just as Peter did.

There are situations in which you find yourself, where you cannot easily carry the Bible or any book to encounter the Word of God. There is also probably not enough time to pray at that time, and no one around to lay hands on you, but you need liberty from the devil's oppression. In such situations, you need to remember that you carry a name that is loaded with the unction required for your rescue — the name of Jesus! With that name, every Goliath before you will come down!

There is an anointing in that name that destroys

yokes, divides the flames of fire and silences death. The use of that name puts you in dominion. That is why the Bible says:

> ***At the name of Jesus every knee should bow, of things in heaven, and things in earth, and things under the earth;***
>
> ***And that every tongue should confess that Jesus Christ is Lord, to the glory of God the Father.***
>
> Philippians 2:10-11

The name of Jesus destroys challenges and brings every opposition down. Every time you are confronted with a challenge, look at it with the eye of faith, and from the depth of your heart release the name of Jesus in faith; that opposition must bow!

The Blood Of Jesus

Theologians tell us that the blood of Jesus only cleanses us from our sins. That is not the whole truth. When the blood came on the scene, see what the Bible says it also did for us:

> ***And they sung a new song, saying, Thou art worthy to take the book, and to open the seals thereof: for thou wast slain, and hast redeemed us to God by thy blood out of every kindred, and tongue, and people, and nation;***
>
> ***And hast made us unto our God kings and priests:***

and we shall reign on the earth.

And I beheld, and I heard the voice of many angels round about the throne and the beasts and the elders: and the number of them was ten thousand times ten thousand, and thousands of thousands;

Saying with a loud voice, Worthy is the Lamb that was slain to receive power, and riches, and wisdom, and strength, and honour, and glory, and blessing.

Revelation 5:9-12

The blood of Jesus, apart from cleansing from sin, also delivered to man power, riches, wisdom, strength, honour, glory and blessing. The blood is also referred to as the blood of the covenant.

The blood of Jesus is the covenant stronghold of the saints. When you have a good understanding of what the blood stands for and its potency, then you will become unstoppable and can no longer be molested by anyone or thing.

As for thee also, by the blood of thy covenant I have sent forth thy prisoners out of the pit wherein is no water.

Turn you to the strong hold, ye prisoners of hope; even today do I declare that I will render double unto thee;

Zechariah 9:11-12

The blood of Jesus is like the sword of a mighty man. When you take cover under the blood (because the life of the flesh is in the blood), the Lord shall be seen over you. Triumph is impossible without the blood. Jesus came to take all power from the devil and give it back to us. All this represents dominion.

> ***And the LORD shall be seen over them, and his arrow shall go forth as the lightning: and the LORD GOD shall blow the trumpet, and shall go with whirlwinds of the south.***
>
> ***The LORD of hosts shall defend them; and they shall devour, and subdue with sling stones; and they shall drink, and make a noise as through wine; and they shall be filled like bowls, and as the corners of the altar.***
>
> Zechariah 9:14-15

As long as you are under this blood cover, you remain impenetrable and inaccessible, because the God of the blood will be seen upon you, and His arrows shall go forth as lighting on your behalf. The blood of the covenant exempts you from molestations, shame and reproach. See your covering and dignity in it, as it wraps you up in power and dominion. It's time to walk in it for your dominion.

The devil's last card is death, and death cannot cross the bloodline. So, it's time to come under the canopy of the blood. Every occultic sect has blood connections, but whatever is from above is above all. No man born of a woman can be compared with Christ in any form. If there is any blood covenant that initiates people into any occultic sect, none can be compared in efficacy with the one that connects us to heaven.

The blood is a missile in heavenly places. It will always hit its' target when invoked in faith. The bold declaration of, "The blood of Jesus!" by any heavenly citizen must work. By destiny, all heavenly citizens are more than conquerors, as Satan is not permitted to prevail in this realm. So begin to use this blood of triumph in whatever conflicts of life you are confronted with, and walk on in dominion.

There is tangible power in the blood, as it is God's last card. It was God's trump card in Egypt, when Pharaoh refused to allow Israel leave the land of captivity. But when the blood came on the scene, Israel marched out of Egypt in dominion and abundance!

The blood of Jesus is the divine provision for man's freedom from every form of satanic corruption. It is what it takes to silence the opposition. It is the ultimate for our victory when applied against the wicked plans of the enemy. You turn on a switch in heaven every time you plead the blood of Jesus, as the blood immediately begins to speak, "Passover". By the blood of Jesus, every evil will pass over you, in Jesus' name!

God revealed in Hebrews 12:24 that we have access in mount Zion, the city of refuge, to the blood of sprinkling that speaks for us. The blood of sprinkling provides a covering for us against the wickedness of Satan. Every time God's people appear in Zion, angels are present, whose only job is to sprinkle the blood of the Lamb, which speaks every good thing for the believer. It speaks healing, peace, protection, provision, fruitfulness, etc. And what's more, it is impenetrable by the avenger of blood.

There is a continuous sprinkling of the blood, twenty-four hours of the day, in Zion. Therefore, whenever a child of God appears there, whether alone or with other believers, he gets sprinkled with the precious blood of the Lamb. So, if the devil comes to you with depression or any form of oppression, just blast the atmosphere with the blood. Declare vehemently, "The blood of Jesus is against you, Satan!" The Blood of Jesus is the seal of our victory in every conflict of life. It enables us to walk in dominion.

Testimonies

There is so much power in testimonies, which the Church of Jesus is ignorant of, and so has not fully utilized it.

> ***And they overcame him by the blood of the Lamb, and by the word of their testimony; and they loved not their lives unto the death.***
>
> Revelation 12:11

The blood and testimonies are instruments of triumph. Testimonies eradicate trials. But what do you find in the Church today? People talking only about the trials they are faced with. To walk in dominion, however, we need to talk more about our testimonies. Hear what Isaiah 8:20 says:

> ***To the law and to the testimony: if they speak not according to this word, it is because there is no light in them.***

Stop talking about trials; instead, talk testimonies! Locate relevant testimonies, wrap them up in the blood, and begin to shoot them as missiles at your targets. David shot testimony arrows at Goliath, and collected Goliath's head (1 Sam. 17:37)! The time has come for you to also collect the heads of all your Goliaths.

The blood of Jesus and testimonies are two powerful weapons commonly used even in heaven. They are overcoming forces that cause the saints to be more than conquerors here on earth. Whenever heavenly citizens invoke the blood and shoot testimony arrows, God's presence is released, and His arrows go into operation, causing them to become an ensign in the land. So, take the blood weapon in your right hand, and testimonies in your left, and your dominion is guaranteed, as no devil can prevail against you.

Friend, we are a people born in due season! These mysteries were hid in time past, even from kings and princes, but have been revealed in our generation, so we can walk on gallantly in dominion! We are dangerously armed saints! God in His infinite mercy has revealed great treasures to us, to establish our dominion here on earth. Wielding these weapons, we have been privileged to see many dead people raised back to life; many homes restored, and shattered lives re-moulded.

With the name of Jesus, His blood and testimonies, you're on your way to the top. No devil can prevail against you with these very powerful weapons in your hand. You're fully armed, so march on in victory and dominion!

The Anointing Oil

The mystery of the anointing oil is another blessing we have seen produce very terrific and mind-blowing results. James 5:14-15 reveals one of the tasks the oil is meant to perform for us:

> ***Is any sick among you? let him call for the elders of the church; and let them pray over him, anointing him with oil in the name of the Lord:***

And the prayer of faith shall save the sick, and the Lord shall raise him up; and if he have committed sins, they shall be forgiven him.

The Bible says, "The Lord shall raise him up." It is the Lord that shall raise him up, not the oil. The Lord who authored the oil, will respond to your obedience to raise the dead, destroy cancer, AIDS, etc.

The anointing oil is not a chemical product. It is the Spirit of God mysteriously put in a bottle, and mysteriously designed to communicate the power of God bodily. It is the power of God in the person of the Holy Spirit, placed in a tangible form in the hand of man to humiliate Satan, making an open show of him. It is God's wisdom for man's rescue! It is the might of God. No gate can be shut against it, as every gate is lifted up at its appearance.

The anointing oil carries mysterious virtue. It is what it takes to be absolutely free, as it destroys all discomforts of life. It is God's standard against every invasion of the enemy.

God introduced the mystery of the anointing oil in Exodus 30:23-31, where He gave Moses details on how it was to be mixed. In 1 Samuel 16:13, we see that it is the Spirit of God.

> ***Then Samuel took the horn of oil, and anointed him in the midst of his brethren: and the Spirit of the Lord came upon David from that day forward...***

David was anointed with oil, but what came upon him was not oil, but the Spirit of the Lord. So the anointing oil is a medium through which the Holy Spirit, the power of God, is invoked to intervene on man's behalf. The Holy Spirit goes into manifestation when the oil is applied.

The anointing oil is God's standard or weapon in your hand, to put the enemy where he belongs — far from you, out of your life, home and affairs (Isa. 59:19). No devil in hell can resist the authority loaded in the anointing oil! Look at what it did in the days of the disciples:

> ***And they went out, and preached that men should repent.***

And they cast out many devils, and anointed with oil many that were sick, and healed them.

Mark 6:12-13

The anointing oil is able to end all frustrations in your life. When it touches the barren, she becomes abundantly fruitful. When it touches anyone chained by the devil, the person becomes automatically free. There is no sickness or disease of any kind that can escape the power in the anointing oil. So, discover the mystery in the anointing oil, and it will put you over always, causing you to walk in dominion!

The Church of Jesus must begin to appropriate the significance and uses of this divine instrument of power, to see the finger of God move supernaturally in the affairs of men. Many have lost grip of what the anointing oil really stands for. Look beyond that common chemical called, "Olive oil", into the mystery that it carries. The anointing oil is not mere oil; there is a person mysteriously packaged inside it. The Holy Ghost is meant to make men comfortable, eradicate hardship and erase affliction. That is what the oil does, as it is the Holy Ghost in a mystery.

Whose fan is in his hand, and he will thoroughly purge his floor, and gather his wheat into the garner; but he will burn up the chaff with

unquenchable fire.

Matthew 3:12

The Holy Ghost has a broom in His hands with which He thoroughly garnishes His floor. He will gather together all the chaff in your life, and burn them up with unquenchable fire. That bottle in your hand is no ordinary liquid, but fire! In other words, its content is highly dangerous. What natural explanation can you give that will justify its catching fire when poured on the ground? The Person inside the oil came alive! Who can shoot an arrow at fire and get results? What kind of knife can you use to cut fire? Can any gun kill it? Everything inherent in the person of the Holy Ghost can be found inside the bottle.

I blessed a bottle of oil for a cousin in 1991, and he kept it away in his wardrobe. His business was about to hit the rocks when suddenly he remembered the oil. He brought it out of his wardrobe, and anointed all his signposts with it, and business immediately picked up for him! The Holy Ghost is THE comforter, not A comforter. There is no situation he cannot handle. Every hardship in life answers to his authority.

Note that we are not only to anoint people with the oil, but can also anoint things. The children of Israel anointed their tabernacle, laver, offerings, etc. with the oil.

> ***And thou shalt anoint the tabernacle of the congregation therewith, and the ark of the testimony,***
>
> ***And the table and all his vessels and the candlestick and his vessels and the altar of incense,***
>
> ***And the altar of burnt offering with all his vessels, and the laver and his foot.***
>
> ***And thou shalt sanctify them, that they may be most holy: whatsoever toucheth them shall be holy.***
>
> ***And thou shalt anoint Aaron and his sons, and consecrate them, that they may minister unto me in the priest's office.***
>
> ***And thou shalt speak unto the children of Israel, saying, This shall be an holy anointing oil unto me throughout your generations.***
>
> Exodus 30:26-31

God has given us a rod; we can't afford to sit down and watch magicians molest us. The Egyptian were rod-less at the end of the first round of conflict with Moses. If Moses had not cast down his rod, would it have become a serpent? Stop carrying the bottle of anointing oil about for fun; use it! It is not enough to be seen carrying the bottle of anointing oil around; you must put it to work. Moses never parted with his rod, as it was his only weapon of defence.

Whenever you sense evil around you, stand to your feet and pour the oil on the ground. Speak to the situation and let it know you are in charge. Let it know power from on high has taken over. Any day you are on your way out and you've left your oil at home, go back for it. Somebody might need your help on the way, and you will be able to manifest your glory.

The man Smith Wigglesworth was a man of one book and one bottle - the Bible and the oil. He died at the age of 87 and never needed to use any form of medicine. Friend, it works! So, why should you continue to suffer whereas you have power in your house? You have the Comforter at your disposal, why must you die in discomfort? There will always be a performance of the things the mouth of the Lord has spoken.

From now on, as you handle this instrument of glory, every discomfort in your life and around you shall become history, in Jesus' name.

The Mantle

It will be recalled that at the time of Elijah's departure, Elisha took up the mantle of Elijah that fell from him. When he got to the bank of Jordan and could not cross over, he smote the waters with the mantle that fell from Elijah, declaring, *"Where is the Lord God of Elijah?"* and the waters parted, and Elisha went over (2 Kgs. 2:13-14).

Any material that has come in contact with the anointed of God carries the unction for manifestation. Such material is what is referred to as the mantle in our context.

God's presence is proved by the manifestations of signs and wonders. The Bible says the disciples went forth and preached everywhere, the Lord working with them, and confirming the Word with signs following (Mk. 16:20). Hebrews 2:4 also tells us: "God also bearing them witness, both with *signs and wonders, and with divers miracles and gifts of the Holy Ghost, according to his own will?"* Therefore, every time you see signs and wonders, know that God is present.

Now let me show you God's wisdom at work. Mark 5:30 tells the story of the woman with the issue of blood. When she touched Jesus, He asked, " Who touched my clothes?" Also in Acts 19:11-12, we are told:

> ***And God wrought special miracles by the hands of Paul:***
>
> ***So that from his body were brought unto the sick***

handkerchiefs or aprons, and the diseases departed from them, and the evil spirits went out of them.

It was not Paul that wrought the special miracles; it was God. The virtue that healed the people did not come out from Paul, but from God. The virtue that operates in the mantle (the handkerchief or clothe from an anointed man of God) is God's virtue. That is why I never feel anything leave my body when miracles take place via the mantle.

One day I was walking through the congregation to the pulpit, and a man who had suffered a spinal injury for seventeen years touched my clothes (a flowing gown) and immediately heard a cracking sound in his lumbar region. That was it! He was instantly healed! And for the first time in seventeen years, he did not need his lumbar jacket anymore. The power of God healed him instantly. It was God's virtue, not mine, because nothing left me when he was healed; unlike Jesus, who felt virtue leave Him when the woman with the issue of blood touched Him.

The virtue in the mantle is from God, not from any prophet or man of God. All we need do is to provoke Him with our obedience. Only then will we see His virtue go into action. Elisha said, *"Where is the Lord God of Elijah?"* and God's virtue went into action. Note that it was not Elijah's virtue, as Elijah was already gone by then (2 Kgs. 2:12-14). Whatever God can handle, his virtue can handle.

"And God wrought special miracles by the hands of Paul..." Those miracles were wrought without any special effort from Paul or the people. The aprons and handkerchiefs they brought from Paul were enough to check out the diseases and evil spirits, but it was God working. The people took notice and acknowledged Paul as a man that had the hand of God upon his life. So when he could not go to where the problem was, they knew they could take anything from him to the problem, and it would be gone.

Friend, God has not changed. He is still working by the hands of men today. These are men who carry transferable unction, and are sent for the deliverance of mankind, the liberty of the captives, the opening of blind eyes, raising the dead, and for the blessing of the people.

In 1989, a brother's wife ran mad in another town that was some distance from where I was. Since I could not go with him to where she was, I took my handkerchief, spoke some powerful words into it, and gave it to him, saying, "Get down to Ekpoma with this, and the power working inside me is going with you now. Wipe her face with this handkerchief when you get there, and the madness will be gone."

He left, believing, and later testified that as soon as the mad woman saw the handkerchief, she ran to grab it, but he held her and wiped her face with it, and the madness vanished instantly! She became pregnant that same month, and nursed her baby all by herself. Till today, she is doing fine in the Lord.

Friend, the mantle of a prophet of God in your hands will work wonders! God gave me this mantle ministry for the liberation of mankind, and we have countless testimonies as proof. The mantle ministry is a ministry of transmission of unction. As I speak forth the anointing for special miracles and casting out of devils to go into the handkerchief (even as Jesus spoke to the fig tree and it heard Him), wherever it appears, the works of the devil will be destroyed. It is a mantle for exploits. It is the end-time prophetic mystery in the hand of the carrier, for amazing results, signs and wonders. It is a carrier of divine energy and heavenly virtue. It always produces signs!

The Communion

I am the living bread which came down from heaven: If any man eat of this bread, he shall live for ever: and the bread that I will give is my flesh, which I will give for the life of the world.

The Jews therefore strove among themselves, saying,

> ***How can this man give us his flesh to eat?***
>
> ***Then Jesus said unto them, Verily, verily, I say unto you, Except ye eat the flesh of the Son of man, and drink his blood, ye have no life in you.***
>
> ***Whoso eateth my flesh, and drinketh my blood, hath eternal life; and I will raise him up at the last day.***
>
> ***For my flesh is meat indeed, and my blood is drink indeed.***
>
> ***He that eateth my flesh, and drinketh my blood, dwelleth in me, and I in him.***
>
> ***As the living Father hath sent me, and I live by the Father: so he that eateth me, even he shall live by me.***
>
> John 6:51-57

The communion is the flesh and the blood of Jesus. We renew our eternal life policy every time we come to the communion table, by contacting the Zoe, the very life of God. When you partake of the communion, whatever flows in Jesus (the vine) begins to flow in you (the branch), causing eternal life to swallow up our human life that is susceptible to demonic oppressions.

There is no drink, capsule or medicine that can be compared with the flesh and blood of Jesus. The communion is a supreme capsule and a supreme injection that cannot be compared with any other. I don't care who your family or specialist doctor is, Jesus said, *"For My flesh is meat indeed, and My blood is drink indeed."*

In the Garden of Eden, God gave Adam and Eve all kinds of shrubs and herbs. For what purpose did He give it to them? It was for food (Gen. 1:29). He never intended for these plants to be for their healing. If only men would eat what God intended for them to eat, they will not experience sickness and disease. When God created man, He never made provisions for his healing; He only gave man what to eat.

It was after man was corrupted and dethroned that Satan's wicked rule and oppression began. God then had to send His only begotten Son with another type of food, designed to make us never need drugs of any kind. What is that food? *"My flesh is meat indeed, and my blood is drink indeed."* If you partake of the communion table with this understanding, you will never need to take any drug for the remaining days of your life!

The breaking of bread (the communion table) is the best hospital to transfer any case to. It is the highest theatre, the office of the Greatest Specialist — Jesus Himself, the Great Physician, the Balm of Gilead! The communion is God's ultimate prescription for our total health.

The apostles continued in the breaking of bread daily, so sickness was far from them.

> ***And they, continuing daily with one accord in the temple, and breaking bread from house to house, did eat their meat with gladness and singleness of heart.***
>
> Acts 2:46

Don't esteem the communion table lightly, as everything you will ever require for your total health is found in it. It will make you live like Jesus here on earth, where Jesus becomes the One working out all things for you, and you operate in His class.

> ***As the living Father hath sent me, and I live by the Father: so he that eateth me, even he shall live by me.***
>
> John 6:57

God said He will satisfy your mouth with good things, and Jesus said, *"I am that bread of life...that cometh down from heaven, that a man may eat thereof, and not die."* Nothing compares in value with the nutritious value found in the flesh and blood of Jesus! You become spiritually indestructible when you partake of it. Sickness will no longer be mentioned around you. The communion makes it impossible for you to be humiliated or molested health-wise.

Jesus said as often as you observe this ordinance, you remember Him:

> ***For I have received of the Lord that which also I delivered unto you, That the Lord Jesus, the same night in which he was betrayed took bread:***
>
> ***And when he had given thanks, he brake it, and said, Take, eat; this is my body, which is broken for you: this do in remembrance of me.***
>
> ***After the same manner also he took the cup, when he had supped, saying, This cup is the new testament in my blood: this do ye, as oft as ye drink it, in remembrance of me.***
>
> ***For as often as ye eat this bread, and drink this cup, ye do shew the Lord's death till he come.***
>
> 1 Corinthians 11:23-26

The communion takes care of everything that weakens you and mocks your redemptive testimony. The children of Israel ate manna in the wilderness, and as they went from nation to nation, from one people to the other, God suffered no man to manhandle them. He cursed kings for their sakes, saying, *"Touch not mine anointed and do my prophets no harm" (Ps. 105:13-15).*

The communion makes it impossible for any devil to harm you. Would Jesus suffer what you're suffering right now? If your answer is no, as you take the communion, say an angry and eternal "No!" to whatever you are going through right now, and it will never reoccur in your life again.

The communion infuses God's kind of life into your blood stream, bones, marrows, mind and spirit-man. It instantly destroys whatever is contrary to life inside your system. It's a mystery, an end-time wisdom of God for your dominion. It is for the saints, for the Church of Jesus Christ. So, use it!

Feet Washing

The feet washing mystery is, among other things, God's wisdom for establishing the dominion of the saints. The second Adam brought back for us what was lost through the first Adam.

> ***Jesus knowing that the Father had given all things into his hands, and that he was come from God, and went to God;***
>
> ***He riseth from supper, and laid aside his garments; and took a towel, and girded himself.***
>
> ***After that he poureth water into a bason, and began to wash the disciples' feet, and to wipe them with the towel wherewith he was girded.***
>
> ***Then cometh he to Simon Peter: and Peter saith unto him, Lord, dost thou wash my feet?***

> ***Jesus answered and said unto him, What I do thou knowest not now; but thou shalt know hereafter.***
>
> ***Peter saith unto him, Thou shalt never wash my feet. Jesus answered, If I wash thee not, thou hast no part with me.***
>
> John 13:3-8

By this mysterious exercise of feet washing, Jesus was restoring to the new generation of human race (the new creation) the dominion that was lost in the first Adam. So, as your feet are dipped into water, you step into the plan of God, through the mysteries of His wisdom, and walk into the realm of dominion. If all things given to Jesus are handed over to you, tell me what devil will ever be able to challenge you?

Jesus washed His disciples' feet so they too could enter the realm where the Father had put Him. Evidently, dominion was passed onto the disciples through this mystery of divine transference, such that when Jesus left, they represented Him, spirit, soul and body. Everything bowed to them, just as they did to Jesus.

From now on, as you observe this ordinance, every evil will bow before you, and whatever part in Christ that you are yet to experience will be delivered unto you. For example, you certainly need unbeatable intelligence in the things of God, so you can run the affairs of this life. It will be delivered to you via this mystery. Jesus had such amazing wisdom that sounded in heaven and answered here on earth also. The same Jesus said to us, *"The works that I do you shall do, and greater works shall you do"* (Jn. 14:12). Your inheritance of the Jesus order of wisdom shall be delivered to you, in Jesus' name!

Friend, there's a part you have in Christ that Satan is out to keep away from you. Now you know it, so violently possess your possession by using this great instrument God has delivered to you. The wisdom of feet washing offers you the singular opportunity of stepping into all things delivered to Christ. Don't allow your confidence to be dampened by any devil.

The feet washing mystery is simply God's wisdom on display. What do people stand to gain from it? They will gain their complete inheritance in Christ. And what is this inheritance all about? Mysterious dominion for mysterious triumphs! It is time to resume our rightful positions in redemption.

Chapter 6

Enjoying Financial Dominion

God has also given the Church power for wealth, to enable her walk in financial dominion. But like all God's provision, you need to know how to access it. Financial dominion can only be attained through the giving grace.

> ***But thou shalt remember the Lord thy God: for it is he that giveth thee power to get wealth, that he may establish his covenant which he sware unto thy fathers, as it is this day.***
>
> Deuteronomy 8:18

The power to get wealth is a product of the giving

power. Jesus said in John 10:17:

> ***Therefore doth my Father love me, because I lay down my life, that I might take it again.***

Power to lay down is what provokes power to receive. For example, God could only receive other sons to glory after His first-born Son, Jesus, had first laid down His life. Likewise, there is yet the power that enables you to lay things down. It is the giving power. It is the secret behind the power to get wealth. Until the power to lay things down begins to work in your life, the power to receive will not go into motion.

There is nothing called rain in the atmosphere. The moisture that evaporates from the earth is what forms rain. The reason you have a lot of rainfall along the coast is because there is a continuous evaporation from the sea. Once moisture gets to a particular height, it condenses, and as soon as the atmosphere can no longer hold it, it falls down as rain. Rainfall is a product of evaporation.

In the same vain, if nothing first goes up from you, don't expect anything to come down to you. Some find it difficult to give because they have not yet received this power. When the power to lay down comes upon them, they will no longer feel the pinch of sacrifice. This is the force behind plenty and financial dominion.

Therefore, as ye abound in everything, in faith, and utterance, and knowledge, and in all diligence, and in your love to us, see that ye abound in this grace also.

2 Corinthians 8:7

Paul was referring to the giving grace here.

Moreover, brethren, we do you to wit of the grace of God bestowed on the churches of Macedonia;

How that in a great trial of affliction the abundance of their joy and their deep poverty abounded unto the riches of their librality.

For to their power, I bear record, yea, and beyond their power they were willing of themselves;

Praying us with much entreaty that we would receive the gift, and take upon us the fellowship of the ministering to the saints.

2 Corinthians 8:1-4

There is a grace made available to every believer, that makes laying down what we have cheap and sweat less. This was the grace upon the Macedonian Church. It provides an open access into the realm of glorious riches for you. Even in the midst of trials, this grace could not be subdued in them.

Somebody once asked me, "What do you do between the time you give and the time you receive?" My reply was, "This is the first time I will ever give that a thought!" This is because Ecclesiastes 11:3 says, *"If the clouds be full of rain, they empty themselves upon the earth."* So, once your cloud is full of giving, your rain of abundance will fall. No devil can stop it.

Some Christians never get to experience their rainfall of abundance until their journey here on earth is over, because the power to lay down is not at work in their lives. The giving power always precedes the receiving power. He that gives sparingly will also receive sparingly, while he that gives bountifully will receive bountifully (2 Cor. 9:6). This is heaven's commandment and policy, and it is the shortest cut to walking in financial dominion.

Givers are winners and rulers. If you're a giver, God prunes you; thereby doing away with all the parasites called fever, headache, etc. so you can bear more fruits (Jn. 15:2). God cuts off every trouble that would have disturbed and made life uncomfortable for giving saints, so they can bear more fruits.

You will never come across a Christian who enjoys plenty who doesn't have plenty of power to lay down.

Moisture does not need to be prayed for before it becomes rain. As long as it is enough, it condenses and comes down as rain. David gave with all his might, and experienced a deluge of the rain of abundance. Solomon gave a thousand burnt offerings, and the heavens opened for him. Abraham gave and gave, until he gave to one man that had no descendant - Melchizedek, the Jesus of the Old Testament. God also gave and gave, until He gave His only Son.

So many Christians today are looking for power to receive, but have not yet received the power to first lay down. They go from North Pole to South Pole, looking for financial abundance. But we must remember that it is the blessing of the Lord that makes rich, and that by strength shall no man prevail.

There are some fellows today, who once they lay their hands on some big money, begin to negotiate their tithe. You will recall that until Solomon finished building the house of the Lord, he didn't build his own house. If you do what God has commanded you to do, you will stop going around in circles.

He has said that giving is the way to financial dominion, and has also released the giving grace to enable you actualize it. So, receive that grace today, and begin to walk in financial dominion, in Jesus' name! From now on, with joy and gladness, you will be more than willing to give to God and the suffering world, thereby establishing your dominion over money, in Jesus precious name!

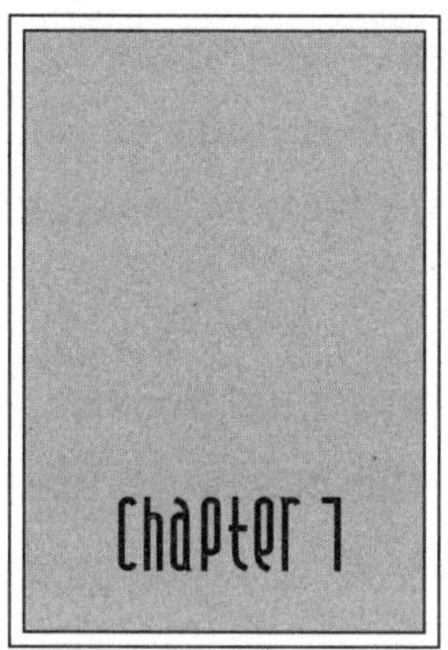

The Gospel Channel

Let me show you another secret for walking in dominion. This secret channel of power has been greatly unexplored. It is the gospel channel. Apostle Paul said:

> ***For I am not ashamed of the gospel of Christ: for it is the power of God unto salvation to every one that believeth; to the Jew first, and also to the Greek.***
>
> Romans 1:16

One of the most hidden sources of power is the gospel. The gospel is so powerful that you must first receive power before you can proclaim it.

> ***But ye shall receive power after that the Holy Ghost***

is come upon you: and ye shall be witnesses unto me both in Jerusalem, and in all Judea, and in Samaria, and unto the uttermost part of the earth.

Acts 1:8

Until you start proclaiming the gospel, you have not yet arrived in the power realm. You are initiated into this realm when you are baptised in the Holy Ghost, but you walk in its inherent power by proclaiming the gospel. Note that everyone that is baptised in the Holy Ghost has been ordained a preacher. You do not have to be a pastor or an evangelist to proclaim the gospel. Preaching the gospel is part of the whole armour of God believers are expected to put on.

And your feet shod with the preparation of the gospel of peace.

Ephesians 6:15

Preaching the good news of Jesus grants you access to dominion, because while you are busy harvesting souls for Christ, you are building yourself up in the realm of power. Special privileges abound to those who preach the gospel. See what Jesus said:

Go ye therefore, and teach all nations, baptizing them in the name of the Father, and of the Son, and

of the Holy Ghost.

Teaching them to observe all things whatsoever I have commanded you: and lo, I am with you alway, even unto the end of the world.

Matthew 28:19-20

You are guaranteed God's presence when you preach the gospel, and we know that with God on your side your dominion is guaranteed. Not only that, the Bible says the disciples went and preached everywhere, and God was working with them, confirming the Word with signs following (Mk. 16:20).

Preaching the gospel is not difficult; neither do you have to go out of your way to do it. Here are a few ways of sharing the good news: for every seemingly simple question anyone asks you, give him a gospel answer. Also give everyone you give a ride the gospel. Every time you write a relation, share the gospel with him or her.

Enter into a covenant with God that no week will pass by without somebody being pulled out of hell by your hands. Whenever you hear someone complain he has a headache, call him and tell him, "Jesus can heal you right now." Next, ask him, "Do you want to be healed?" There is nobody in trouble who is not looking for a solution. Friend, the gospel is power, so market it with all confidence. It is a priceless commodity; go and sell it, and enter the realms of dominion.

The world is suffering and dying, don't keep all the food to yourself and watch her starve to death. It is time for the manifestation of the sons of God; it is time to present the gospel to all and sundry. It is the answer to the needs of mankind.

Proclaiming the gospel is the cheapest way to walk in power and dominion. This is because God is always ready to back up His Word. He said in Psalm 81:10, *"Open thy mouth wide, and I will fill it."* The time has come for us to walk in the realm of power, to such a level that when we walk into any hospital, the sick will begin to rise up from their beds on their own accord!

A lot of Christians think they can acquire power by crying. No! Ephesians 6:15 has told us the way to it: *"And your feet shod with the preparation of the gospel of peace."* When you go about proclaiming the gospel, you find yourself walking about with supernatural shoes on, with which you tread on serpents and scorpions, and over all the power of the enemy, without any hurt (Lk. 10:19). Those who proclaim the gospel are always heavily protected. They are also heavily defended, because they have supernatural shoes on.

Friend, the power is in your feet! You can't walk in dominion until you walk about proclaiming the gospel. It is a privilege to carry food to the hungry, to bring light to those who are seated in darkness, while at the same time enjoying divine immunity and security.

Let us also consider another angle to proclaiming the gospel. The Bible says:

> ***Death and life are in the power of the tongue: and they that love it shall eat the fruit thereof.***
>
> Proverbs 18:21

There is power built into your tongue, and if you use it in propagating the gospel, which is the power of God unto salvation, you can imagine the amount of power you have at your disposal! It means you are releasing double power when you preach the gospel. When you put the gospel on your tongue, the power of God mixes with the power of the tongue, and you become an explosive among men!

Close–mouthed Christians will remain eternal victims, rather than walk in dominion as they are destined to. It is time to make full use of the power of God available to you. Stand up, and make the devil know he does not have a hold on those lives. This is how to walk in dominion.

The disciples in the early Church were men and women who walked in dominion. But what was their secret? Acts 14:3 tells us:

> ***Long time therefore abode they speaking boldly in the Lord, which gave testimony unto the word of his grace, and granted signs and wonders to be done by their hands.***

The disciples were speaking boldly, and the authorities could not handle them. They were in charge! Proclaiming the gospel makes you a man and woman to be feared.

Aside from all that has been said, there are several other benefits of preaching the gospel. Let us consider some of them:

Signs By Your Hands

> ***And he said unto them, Go ye into all the world, and preach the gospel to every creature.***
>
> ***He that believeth and is baptized shall be saved; but he that believeth not shall be damned.***
>
> ***And these signs shall follow them that believe; In my name shall they cast out devils; they shall speak with new tongues.***
>
> Mark 16:15-17

Signs follow people; they do not just drop on them. Until you are on the go preaching the gospel, you will not see signs. Once you are on the go, the name of Jesus will begin to produce results for you. Your duty is to go out and preach; leave God, the Lord of the harvest, to bring in the harvest of men.

Everybody is looking for a way of escape. It is indeed a great privilege that you have already escaped. So go forth, and become a miracle worker, bringing the good news of the gospel to those who are perishing. Jesus did not experience the first miracle in His ministry while sitting in His house. No! He was on the move, and He manifested His glory in Cana of Galilee. One of the greatest benefits you enjoy therefore, as you go around lifting people out of their problems, is the manifestation of signs by your hands (Mk. 16:20).

The Word of God is a consuming fire; and signs always follow those who preach the Word. If your life is void of signs and wonders, it is because you are not on the move, proclaiming the gospel. Signs are for men in motion. If you are not on the move, you won't see them. You cannot sit at a place and expect signs to follow you.

Start teaching, preaching and giving people gospel solutions to their afflictions, and signs will keep following you. You won't become a miracle worker until you become a gospel preacher.

You Enjoy God's Presence

And they went forth, and preached everywhere, the Lord working with them, and confirming the word with signs following.

Mark 16:20

When you become a carrier of the gospel, God places His seal upon your life, and His presence is compelled to follow you. And if God be for you, who can be against you?

And Jesus came and spake unto them, saying, All power is given unto me in heaven and in earth.

Go ye therefore, and teach all nations, baptizing them in the name of the Father, and of the Son and of the Holy Ghost:

Teaching them to observe all thing whatsoever I have commanded you: and, lo, I am with you alway, even unto the end of the world.

Matthew 28:18-20

God is with the preacher of the gospel always. What happens when God is with you? Obstacles give way to miracles of course! Psalm 114:1-4 recounts:

When Israel went out of Egypt, the house of Jacob

from a people of strange language;

Judah was his sanctuary, and Israel his dominion.

The sea saw it, and fled: Jordan was driven back.

The mountains skipped like rams, and the little hills like lambs.

What ailed thee, O thou sea, that thou fleddest? thou Jordan, that thou wast driven back?

When God is with you, obstacles give way to you. You tread upon serpents and scorpions, and over all the power of the enemy, and nothing shall by any means hurt you.

If you are not a gospel bearer, you are running a risk, as one great thing sharing the gospel does for you is that it guarantees God's presence with you. You become a God–carrier when you become a gospel bearer. You cannot enjoy the fullness of God's blessings without carrying the gospel. God's presence is more than enough to keep you afloat. Note that it's not just His presence, but His presence coupled with signs following. That is dominion!

Every time you speak God's Word, He's on the spot to watch over it and see that signs follow. So, it's time to go about fully armed with the gospel. Bearing the gospel is spiritual armory.

You Earn Wages

And he that reapeth receiveth wages...

John 4:36

Many of us have been giving our money in order to receive. But there is yet another way we can earn wages. It is by proclaiming the gospel. Heaven pays you wages for every soul you rescue soul from death. The Bible says:

For what is a man profited, if he shall gain the whole world, and lose his own soul? or what shall a man give in exchange for his soul?

Matthew 16:26

To God, one soul has more value than all the resources of the world put together. The value of a job is what determines how much you pay the one who does it. Preaching the gospel is of great value, so let's go out and tell the world that Jesus makes the difference in any life, and that He's the reason we are smiling. As people tell you all manner of trials they are going through, you must in turn tell them the gospel truth, which they need for their escape.

Everyone that comes to you, complaining about what is going on in his life is looking for a solution. Present him with one – the gospel solution. As you do so, you are rescuing a soul from death, and at the same time increasing your heavenly account.

Protection And Defence

> ***And they that be wise shall shine as the brightness of the firmament; and they that turn many to righteousness, as the stars for ever and ever.***
>
> Daniel 12:3

It is wisdom to proclaim the gospel and see others plucked out of the fire, rescued from death, and brought out of the dungeon. Not only is it wisdom to proclaim the gospel and lead many to Christ by providing answers to the questions of suffering humanity; more than that, it guarantees you heaven's protection and defence.

The gospel is good news. Everyone that goes about proclaiming it is doing a good thing. First Peter 3:13 asks, *"And who is he that will harm you, if ye be followers of that which is good?"* Therefore, no one can harm you as you go about proclaiming the gospel. Indeed, it guarantees your protection, as you are empowered to tread upon serpents and scorpions, and over all the power of the enemy, and nothing shall by any means hurt you. If you make it a lifestyle to get others out of trouble, you will never be in trouble yourself. And if you rescue others from death, you will not die.

We serve a God of seedtime and harvest. If you are the reason for the joy of somebody else, you will never become a victim of sorrow. If you are responsible for someone else's feeding, you'll never become a beggar on the earth. Matthew 6:33 says:

> ***But seek ye first the kingdom of God, and his righteousness; and all these things shall be added unto you.***

What is the kingdom of God in this context? It is simply people coming to Christ. Every part you play in drawing people into the kingdom is an investment that will bring you out of affliction when you need it.

You Enjoy Sound Health

> ***Every branch in me that beareth not fruit he taketh away: and every branch that beareth fruit, he purgeth it, that it may bring forth more fruit.***
>
> John 15:2

Another major benefit of preaching the gospel is that you enjoy sound health. If you are busy proclaiming the truth of the gospel of Jesus, then you are automatically entitled to enjoy divine health.

The man of God, Kenneth E. Hagin, said that for 63 years he never had as much as a headache! Even in his 80s, he was still able to attend preaching engagements where he conducted three services a day! This is because everyone who proclaims the gospel automatically lives a healthy life. *"He that beareth fruit I will prune."* God is simply saying here, *"I will make you healthy, so you can bear more fruit."*

Lester Sumrall said, "I am 83 years old, and I'm perfectly healthy. I use no medication of any sort." You cannot be a part of the solution to men's problems and remain a problem yourself. Let's stop looking at the dying world; let's rescue them from destruction. It is time to pull people away from the jaws of the lion.

I used to be very sickly as a young lad. I was no better than a weakling. But today, I am as strong as a lion! Even when I do not feel like working, I just find myself doing something. It is a privilege to be a workman for Jesus. We see people healed, delivered and pulled out of hell in our ministry everyday.

God has given an assurance that as long as you are part of setting other people free, He will never watch you remain in any form of bondage. So, go out with your feet shod with the preparation of the gospel of peace, and walk in dominion!

The Holy Ghost Power

But ye shall receive power, after that the Holy Ghost is come upon you...

Acts 1:8

You need the Holy Ghost power to walk in total dominion. The Holy Ghost power is like the icing on the cake, that holds all that we have discussed together. It is impossible to walk in dominion without this power. That was why Jesus said to His disciples:

...But tarry ye in the city of Jerusalem, until ye be endued with power from on high.

Luke 24:49

Jesus knew His disciples needed this power to be able to do anything. And that power came down in the form of the Holy Ghost in Acts chapter 2.

> ***And when the day of Pentecost was fully come, they were all with one accord in one place.***
>
> ***And suddenly there came a sound from heaven as of a rushing mighty wind, and it filled all the house where they were sitting.***
>
> ***And there appeared unto them cloven tongues like as of fire, and it sat upon each of them***
>
> ***And they were all filled with the Holy Ghost, and began to speak with other tongues, as the Spirit gave them utterance.***
>
> Acts 2:1-4

When you receive the baptism of the Holy Ghost, you receive a baptism of power. You are born into power at salvation, and baptised into power by the Holy Ghost. There is no reason, therefore, for you to live a defeated life.

When you enter into the power region, you become a power-packed creature. You are backed up from heaven with the power of God. This power is not just an emblem, but an instrument of dominion (Lk. 10:19).

It Is In Levels

Note that the power of the Holy Ghost manifests

at various levels in people's lives, depending on how much room they allow Him in their lives. Some are just saved and enjoying the well level, while others are filled with the Holy Ghost at the river level. Yet others are at the anointing level, and are enjoying the rain of the Holy Ghost.

When you are born again, you operate from a spiritual dimension that can be likened to a well of water level. Jesus told the Samaritan woman in John 4:14:

> ***But whosoever drinketh of the water that I shall give him shall never thirst; but the water that I shall give him shall be in him a well of water springing up into everlasting life.***

The water here represents the Holy Spirit. But speaking at the feast in *John 7:38-39*, Jesus said:

> ***He that believeth on me, as the scripture hath said, out of his belly shall flow rivers of living water.***
>
> ***(But this spake he of the Spirit, which they that believe on him should receive: for the Holy Ghost was not yet given; because that Jesus was not yet glorified.)***

Jesus was speaking here of the baptism in the Holy Ghost. The Holy Spirit is in you at a well of water level at salvation. But it graduates to a river level at baptism. You cannot compare a river to a well. A river can generate hydroelectricity, provide water for irrigation, and you can also fish in it. A well on the other hand, cannot produce all these for you, and is also highly subject to climatic conditions. And if the condition gets too harsh, the water in it will dry up. But whatever condition that will dry up all the water in a river, will make life almost impossible in such an environment. When a man or woman is not filled with the Holy Ghost, he or she lacks the resistance required to ward off all attacks of the enemy.

But the river level is not the end. God's Word gives us an understanding of yet another dimension of power, likened to rain.

> ***Ask ye of the Lord rain in the time of the latter rain; so the Lord shall make bright clouds, and give them showers of rain, to every one grass in the field.***
>
> Zechariah 10:1

In Acts chapter 4, the Bible records that where the apostles were praying shook, and they were all filled with the Holy Ghost. This is the rain dimension of power. The only way to fill up a river is by rainfall.

We can, therefore, see the Holy Ghost clearly in three dimensions:

- The well of water level (at salvation)

- The river level (Holy Ghost baptism)
- The rain level (also referred to as the anointing)

One will feel refreshed after attending an anointing service, even if one is not baptised in the Holy Spirit. But you must not mistake this for the baptism of the Holy Spirit. When rain falls, both the well and the river are equally replenished; but a well will never become a river simply because rain fell. In hydroelectricity supply, when the water level is low, the power supply is also reduced, and power is rationed as a result. Likewise, the amount of water (Holy Ghost) in your river determines the amount of power you will generate as a believer.

Understand that these things don't just happen; they are made to happen. You must consciously repent and be born again to enter the well water level of power. To be baptized in the Holy Spirit, on the other hand, you need to believe. Jesus said, *"He that believeth on* me, out of his belly shall flow rivers of living water" (Jn. 7:38). That was why Cornelius' family did not have time to pray before the Holy Ghost fell upon them. As they heard the Word and believed it, they were instantly baptised in the Holy Ghost (Acts 10:44-45). Prayer is your access into the rain level, which is the anointing of the Holy Spirit.

Many might be asking themselves, "What next? We are baptised in the Holy Ghost, we are full of power." But we have seen that power is in levels. The more you grow in it, the more authority you are able to exercise. I want you to increase your thirst for power, which is the major requirement for its release. There has to be a genuine thirst for power on your inside.

The evangelicals will tell you, "Once you are born again, there is no need to be baptised in the Holy Ghost. No one can say Jesus is Lord except by the Holy Ghost." This is talking about a measure of the Spirit of God, and a very dangerous level that won't guarantee you triumph always. It can only succeed in enlisting your name in the book of life. In Acts chapter 2, the apostles were baptised in the Holy Ghost. Yet when they were faced with a challenge in chapter 4, they still needed to pray, and the Bible records that they were filled with the Holy Ghost (Acts 4:31).

What were they filled with the first time? It was with the Holy Ghost. But they received another measure or level of the Holy Ghost in Acts 4. Many of us feel that because we are filled with the Holy Ghost and speak in tongues, that we have reached our peak.

When you receive the Holy Ghost baptism, you are only initiated into the school of the Spirit, where lessons for growth in the spirit realm begin. Ezekiel 47:3-5 shows us different levels of the anointing we can grow into:

> ***And when the man that had the line in his hand went forth eastward, he measured a thousand cubits, and he brought me through the waters; the waters were to the ankles.***
>
> ***Again he measured a thousand, and brought me through the waters; the waters were to the knees, Again he measured a thousand, and brought me through; the waters were to the loins.***
>
> ***Afterward he measured a thousand; and it was a river that I could not pass over: for the waters were risen, waters to swim in, a river that could not be passed over.***

There is the ankle length level of anointing, the knee and loins level, and finally, a river that cannot be passed over level. Make your choice!

Jesus promised that He was going to His Father and would send the Holy Ghost to us when He got there. Jesus is now seated at the right hand of the Father and Ezekiel 47 tells us that the water flows from the right side of the throne. This is a picture of the outpouring of the anointing of the Holy Spirit upon the end-time Church.

Jesus is still sending the Holy Spirit as He promised, and we can enjoy the outpouring at various measures. If the Holy Ghost does not come, your fullness will never be realised. Let Him have His way, and the Lord will give showers of rain. The world is about to witness the greatest of all moves, and our principal instrument for manifestation is the Holy Ghost at work in our lives.

Our access into God's promised golden phase of life i.e dominion is the anointing of the Holy Spirit. Jesus the Messiah came to this earth, and had no impact until the Holy Ghost came upon Him (Matt. 3:16). For thirty years, He was just the son of Joseph, the carpenter. But after the Holy Ghost came upon Him, His prominence was established. Luke 4:14 tells us:

> ***And Jesus returned in the power of the Spirit into Galilee: and there went out a fame of him through all the region round about.***

That was dominion! Behind exploits in the kingdom is the anointing of the Holy Spirit. In Luke 24:49, Jesus said to His disciples:

> ***...Tarry ye in the city of Jerusalem, until ye be endued***

with power from on high.

You will never make meaning on this earth as a Christian until you are endued with power from on high. You will not go places or walk in dominion until you are endued with the power that only the Holy Spirit gives.

When the Holy Spirit came upon the disciples in Acts 2, they exploded with power, and went from there and turned their world upside down! God has also programmed you for a covenant explosion, so you need to receive the "bomb" of heaven, so you can explode effectively and your position in the kingdom will be established.

There is a golden vision about your life (Zech. 4:2), but you need an outpouring of the Spirit upon you to bring it to pass. You have all the principles; but you now need the power to make it work. Jesus taught the disciples the principles for three and a half years. Yet He told them, "Don't go anywhere yet, it won't work. Get the power from on high first."

We are in the age of attraction for the body of Christ, but it's not going to be by power or by might, but *"by my Spirit, saith the Lord God of hosts."* So, I'd like you to hunger and thirst for the outpouring of that power upon your life; it will compel everything around you to start working. The unction of the Holy Spirit is what guarantees motion in life. Without the Holy Spirit, you can go nowhere. All you will succeed in doing is only going around in circles. But when He comes upon you, explosion will follow. I see an explosion coming upon your life in this new move, in Jesus precious name!

Greater Works! Greater Works!

Concerning those that believe in Him, Jesus said in John 14:12, *"Greater works than these shall he do."* If Jesus could say we shall do greater works than He did, then we have not seen anything yet! But then, exploit is impossible without the Holy Spirit. Until you receive unction, you cannot function. You are going to do greater works, yes; but you first need the unction to function to come upon you. Without the anointing of the Holy Spirit, it will be impossible to have exploits and walk in dominion.

This is because you cannot make impact until you are empowered. If Jesus could not perform without it, neither can you and I. For 30 years His Messianic ministry had no expression, as it were, until unction came upon Him. The Holy Spirit is our surety for dominion and exploits. I see God enduing you with power to perform now, in Jesus' mighty name!

The Rain Of Righteousness, First!

Let me state here, however, that it is impossible to encounter the outpouring of the Spirit, until righteousness is first in place. You cannot have the rain of the Spirit without first having had the rain of righteousness. The rain of righteousness prepares the ground for the rain of the Spirit and the different other kinds of rain. That's why the Bible says:

> ***Turn you at my reproof: behold, I will pour out my spirit unto you, I will make known my words unto you.***
>
> Proverbs 1:23

Until righteousness is in place, you cannot enjoy the outpouring of the Spirit of God. Unction is a function of consecration, not only of prayer. The unction of the Holy Spirit answers only to your personal consecration. By unction I mean, substantial, tangible, and effectual power. Anybody can speak in tongues, but I'm talking about power in demonstration, the type that establishes your dominion here on earth. Paul refers to it as the *"demonstration of the Spirit and of power"* (1 Cor. 2:4). This kind answers only to personal consecration.

Christian Harfourche, in his book *The Miracle*

Ministry of the Prophets said, "I believe with all my heart that there is a certain level of unction that cannot come without the love of righteousness and the hatred of iniquity." This was true with Jesus. Psalm 45:7 says concerning Him:

> ***Thou lovest righteousness, and hatest wickedness: therefore God, thy God, hath anointed thee with the oil of gladness above thy fellows.***

That is talking about unction, which is a direct function of consecration. Righteousness determined the unction that Jesus carried. John's gospel tells us that God gave Him the Spirit without measure (Jn. 3:34), because He had holiness and purity without measure.

It is consecration that determines unction. So it takes the rain of righteousness to enjoy the rain of the Spirit. No wonder Peter told the people in Acts 3:19:

> ***Repent ye therefore, and be converted, that your sins may be blotted out, when the times of refreshing shall come from the presence of the Lord.***

That is the rain of the Spirit. When you repent and are converted, and your sins are blotted out, then you begin to enjoy the times of refreshing that comes by the outpouring of the Spirit. Everyone has a measure of unction, but your level of consecration is what determines the level of unction that God makes available to you. So, the rain of the Spirit is available, but you need an encounter with the rain of righteousness first, to have it.

We are in the greatest hour of opportunity in the body of Christ; we are in the days of His power. Those who are correctly positioned in God are those who will manifest their sonship by walking in dominion. You shall not miss your place in this move!

Operating The Seven Spirits Of God

Apart from being baptized in the Holy Ghost and growing to the anointing level, you also need the seven Spirits of God fully operating in your life to truly walk in dominion. Jesus had the anointing without measure, and also had the seven Spirits of God fully operational in His life.

But what are the seven Spirits of God? Upon who do they come?

And out of the throne proceeded lightnings and

thunderings and voices: and there were seven lamps of fire burning before the throne, which are the seven Spirits of God.

Revelation 4:5

And unto the angel of the church in Sardis write; These things saith he that hath the seven Spirits of God, and the seven stars...

Revelation 3:1

We understand that Jesus is the One speaking to the seven churches here. So He is the One that has the seven Spirits of God. A careful look at the army of the Lord described in Joel 2 reveals something interesting also. Verse 3 says, *"A fire devoureth before them; and behind them a flame burneth."* And by that operation, the land before them was like the garden of Eden, and behind them a desolate wilderness. *"Yea and nothing shall escape them."*

This great army of the Lord will operate by the power of the seven Spirits of God, because we are told in Revelation 4 that out of the throne proceeded lightnings and thunderings and voices, burning before the throne, which are the seven spirits of God.

Also look at Revelation 5:6:

And I beheld, and, lo, in the midst of the throne and of the four beasts, and in the midst of the elders,

stood a Lamb as it had been slain, having seven horns and seven eyes, which are the seven Spirits of God sent forth into all the earth.

Who is that Lamb? Jesus! He has the seven Spirits of God, which are now made available to the sons of God on earth. Those seven Spirits were fully operational in Christ — a pointer to the fact that God wants them to be operational in us too. And when those seven Spirits are at work in a man, he will be nothing but a sign and a wonder on the earth.

We are entitled to the seven Spirits of God in our lives. This is because we can't come into the fullness of the stature of Christ if the forces working in Him are not working in us as well. I see you gain access into the operations of the seven Spirits of God, in the name of Jesus!

But what are the seven Spirits of God?

And there shall come forth a rod out of the stem of Jesse, and a Branch shall grow out of his roots:

And the spirit of the LORD shall rest upon him, the spirit of wisdom and understanding, the spirit of counsel and might, the spirit of knowledge and of the fear of the LORD;

And shall make him of quick understanding in the fear of the LORD: and he shall not judge after the

sight of his eyes, neither reprove after the hearing of his ears:

Isaiah 11:1-3

This is the sum total of the seven spirits of God. They are for a total disarming of wickedness, and the establishment of the peaceful dominion of the Church here on earth. Don't you know He's coming to rapture a Church without spot, wrinkle or anything of such? So He must send us help (that is, supernatural ability) to live above board.

The Spirit Of The Lord

In Luke 4:18 Jesus proclaimed:

The Spirit of the Lord is upon me, because he hath anointed me to preach the gospel to the poor; he hath sent me to heal the brokenhearted, to preach deliverance to the captives, and recovering of sight to the blind, to set at liberty them that are bruised.

This was where the Spirit of the Lord opened the first chapter of the former rain. The other forces are reserved for the last days. It is interesting to note that the former rain brought gifts of the Holy Spirit. First Corinthians chapter 12 tells us that it's all by the same Spirit. That means all the gifts of the Holy Ghost (the nine gifts - faith, healing, working of miracles, prophecy, discerning of spirits, divers kinds of tongues, interpretation of tongues, word of wisdom and word of knowledge) are gifts of the Spirit of the Lord. These all add up to the Spirit of power.

When the Holy Spirit came in Acts chapter 2, He came as the power from on high. The former rain was thus heralded as the power from on high, which is one of the seven Spirits of God. God is omnipotent. So inside Him must be a force that generates power. So the Spirit of the Lord, as it were, stands for the power in the former rain.

> ***And, behold, I send the promise of my Father upon you: but tarry ye in the city of Jerusalem, until ye be endued with power from on high.***
>
> Luke 24:49

One of the key manifestations of the Holy Ghost in the last days is power. When Jesus came on His Messianic assignment to the earth, He came in the spirit of power, to deliver the captives. Luke 4:14 tells us:

> ***And Jesus returned in the power of the Spirit into Galilee: and there went out a fame of him through all the region round about.***

Jesus began to walk in dominion as soon as the Spirit of the Lord came upon Him. He entered the synagogue in Nazareth, and read Isaiah 61:1-2 from the book that was delivered unto Him (Lk. 4:18). When you put Luke 4:14 and 18 together, you will discover that the Spirit of the Lord He was talking about is also the Spirit of power. The Bible says He returned in the power of the Spirit into Galilee, and announced, *"The Spirit of the Lord is upon me."* Therefore, the Spirit of the Lord is the Spirit of power.

The gift of the Holy Spirit is the power from on high. Jesus told the disciples in Acts 1:8:

> ***But ye shall receive power, after that the Holy Ghost is come upon you: and ye shall be witnesses unto me both in Jerusalem, and in all Judaea, and in Samaria, and unto the uttermost part of the earth.***

I'd like you to be thirsty for the impartation of power. You need it to walk in dominion. Jesus said, *"The Spirit of the Lord is upon me, because he hath anointed me..."* To anoint means to empower. That is to say, *"He hath (empowered) me to preach the gospel to the poor..."*

"What is this power for?" you might ask. It is for subduing the enemy.

> ***The Lord said unto my Lord, Sit thou at my right hand, until I make thine enemies thy footstool.***
>
> ***The Lord shall send the rod of thy strength out of Zion: rule thou in the midst of thine enemies.***

> ***Thy people shall be willing in the day of thy power, in the beauties of holiness from the womb of the morning: thou hast the dew of thy youth.***
>
> Psalm 110:1-3

The Spirit of power you are endued with is for subduing the enemy. It is so you can dominate the region of darkness, and say to Satan, "You are no longer in charge here. Your judgment is sealed already." The Spirit of power is to enable you rule over your enemy, Satan, so he cannot bring sickness and failure to you or stand in your way when you are on the move. Satan cannot stop your progress; neither can any witch challenge your destiny. That is the essence of the Spirit of power. It is to make you walk in dominion here on earth!

We see from the above scripture that Jesus will not come until all His enemies are made His footstool. That means God will bring about the outpouring of His power in the last days, such as has never been before. That power will completely disarm all wickedness, subdue kingdoms, and wrought righteousness (Heb. 11:33). There will be strange manifestations in the last days, to totally subdue the enemies of God. Romans 8:19 tells us that the whole creature is waiting for us, because we are in the days of His power.

When the Spirit of power breaks forth on you, you will become a recognised master anywhere you are found. How can you have an All–Powerful, Omnipotent Father and still be a weakling? Where did you get your weakness? From this day, the enemy will not humiliate your destiny anymore!

To truly walk in dominion, however, you must be conscious of the fact that you are loaded with power from on high. That same power is what was at work in Peter, Paul, and other great men of exploits we have read about. If you are baptised with the Holy Ghost, then that same power resides inside you. But until you are conscious of His indwelling presence, you are not yet set for exploits.

From henceforth, anywhere you see the devil trying to make noise, step in and shut him up in the name of Jesus. As you step in, he must step out, because the power of heaven (the Holy Ghost Himself) is resident in you. The whole creation is groaning and travailing in pains, waiting for the sons of God to show up and bring their deliverance. You have what they need, so go forth and manifest your sonship! By the Spirit of power, there will be a total disarming of wickedness, and an establishment of the peaceful dominion of the Church.

The Spirit Of Wisdom

The Lord by wisdom hath founded the earth; by understanding hath he established the heavens.

Proverbs 3:19

O Lord, how manifold are thy works! In wisdom hast thou made them all: the earth is full of thy riches.

Psalm 104:24

All the exploits of the Father God are tied to the wisdom that is operational in Him. It therefore means that for you to be a candidate for His kind of exploits also, you must be connected to His kind of wisdom. Paul the apostle prayed a very special prayer for the Ephesian Church in Ephesians 1:17:

That the God of our Lord Jesus Christ, the Father of glory, may give unto you the spirit of wisdom and revelation in the knowledge of him.

It is God that gives the Spirit of wisdom. But what will it do?

The eyes of your understanding being enlightened; that ye may know what is the hope of his calling, and what the riches of the glory of his inheritance in the saints,

And what is the exceeding greatness of his power to us-ward who believe, according to the working

of his mighty power.

Ephesians 1:18-19

The Spirit of wisdom enlightens your understanding, causing you to know what God has in store for you. It enables you to be mentally productive by illuminating your mind, and imparting you with creative abilities for exploits. It offers strange skills for you to excel in whatever area God has placed you. That is why the Bible says:

I wisdom dwell with prudence, and find out knowledge of witty inventions.

Proverbs 8:12

God's wisdom is creative; so when the Spirit of wisdom is at work in you, you will find heaven just directing you on very mysterious frequencies, to cause you to improve continually on where you are per time. God's wisdom is the ability to form and reform, the ability to create and recreate. We are going to have waves of inventions these last days in the body of Christ, ingenious waves of creativity. Things will just be happening, by reason of God's wisdom at work in His Church. People will begin laying hold on hidden wisdom, to do outstanding exploits.

There will be such strange inventions in our time; the wisdom of God at work in the Church will cause her to burst forth with countless witty inventions! The end-time Church will gain prominence by the many–sided wisdom of God, which only the Holy Spirit imparts.

The Holy Spirit is the One that connects us to the wisdom of God. He teaches us by opening us up to the deep things of God. He helps us out in our quest for knowledge, and reveals truth to our spirit-man. The Holy Spirit cannot teach you and you won't understand what He's teaching you. When He teaches you, He quickens your understanding to grasp the things He is revealing to you.

> ***But God hath revealed them unto us by his Spirit: for the Spirit searcheth all things, yea, the deep things of God.***
>
> ***For what man knoweth the things of a man, save the spirit of man which is in him? even so the things of God knoweth no man, but the Spirit of God.***
>
> ***Now we have received, not the spirit of the world, but the spirit which is of God; that we might know the things that are freely given to us of God.***
>
> ***Which things also we speak, not in the words which man's wisdom teacheth, but which the Holy Ghost teacheth; comparing spiritual things with spiritual.***
>
> 1 Corinthians 2:10-13

God is set to bring a mental revolution to you, by the outpouring of the Holy Spirit. There is a Spirit called the Spirit of wisdom. It is one of the seven Spirits of God, and is delivered to you on request. You cannot operate the Spirit of wisdom and not be creatively productive. There is a better way of doing that job, and a better approach to that assignment. All you need do is to call on Him, to show you the better way, just as Solomon did:

> ***Give me now wisdom and knowledge, that I may go out and come in before this people: for who can judge this thy people, that is so great?***
>
> 2 Chronicles 1:10

It Makes Stars!No one ever gains access to the Spirit of wisdom without becoming a star.

> ***And they that be wise shall shine as the brightness of the firmament; and they that turn many to righteousness, as the stars for ever and ever.***
>
> Daniel 12:3

Their shining will command attention and bring attraction. Note that I'm not talking about the wisdom of this world here. This is not intellectual, technological or scientific wisdom. I'm talking about the wisdom of God in a mystery, which only the Holy Spirit teaches (not the universities and colleges). It is this wisdom that will bring you into the limelight without sweat!

Revelation 5:10 tells us that by the blood of Jesus, we have been redeemed unto God as priests and kings, and we shall reign on the earth. He redeemed you to reign, and it is by wisdom that kings reign, and princes decree justice (Prov. 8:15). You don't have a place in the end-time army without the Spirit of wisdom, because it is a reigning army. So like 1 Corinthians 12:31 counsels, covet this all-important gift.

No one has an encounter with the Spirit of wisdom without making outstanding marks in life. Joseph took over government in Egypt by the Spirit of wisdom. Pharaoh could not help but declare:

> ***...Forasmuch as God hath shewed thee all this, there is none so discreet and wise as thou art:***
>
> ***Thou shalt be over my house, and according unto thy word shall all my people be ruled: only in the throne will I be greater than thou.***
>
> ***And Pharaoh said unto Joseph, See, I have set thee over all the land of Egypt.***
>
> Genesis 41:39-41

The Spirit of wisdom established Joseph's prominence in a strange land. It also established Daniel in a place of prominence among his enemies.

The wisdom at work in him was described as the wisdom of the gods (Dan. 5:11).

Worthy of note is the fact that everyone that operated in the Spirit of wisdom lived a clean life. This is because the Holy Spirit will not relate with filthy men. Daniel lived a clean life. He purposed in his heart not to defile himself (Dan. 1:8). When cornered by Potiphar's wife to lie with him, Joseph said, *"How can I do this great wickedness, and sin against God?"* (Gen. 39:9). They lived extraordinary and very productive lives because of the wisdom of God at work in them. But first of all, they were men of pure of hearts. God said in Proverbs 1:23:

> ***Turn you at my reproof: behold, I will pour out my spirit unto you, I will make known my words unto you.***

You cannot gain access into His wisdom until you have turned at His reproof. No filthy man will ever have access to the Spirit of wisdom. So don't block your access to the throne; leave that sin before it makes a reproach of your life. If you clean up, God promises to beautify you with His wisdom. Then place a demand on God for the release of that Spirit to you. Remember that he that asketh receiveth.

The Spirit Of Understanding

> ***Good understanding giveth favour: but the way of transgressors is hard.***
>
> Proverbs 13:15

There is a Spirit of understanding. It is the excellent Spirit that causes men to excel cheaply. It makes one become outstanding on the earth. It is the ability to intelligibly diagnose situations, put solutions together, and be able to go on to the ultimate end of obtaining practical results. It is knowing what to do to bring situations under control. It is so important that Apostle Paul prayed it for the Ephesian Church:

> ***The eyes of your understanding being enlightened; that ye may know what is the hope of his calling, and what the riches of the glory of his inheritance in the saints.***
>
> Ephesians 1:18

Nothing becomes outstanding without understanding. See how Daniel took over in the land of Babylon. Understanding made him to stand out. He was able to disarm darkness and locate his place in God. See how he was described:

> ***There is a man in thy kingdom, in whom is the spirit of the holy gods; and in the days of thy father light and understanding and wisdom, like the wisdom***

of the gods, was found in him; whom the king Nebuchadnezzar thy father, the king, I say, thy father, made master of the magicians, astrologers, Chaldeans, and soothsayers;

Forasmuch as an excellent spirit, and knowledge, and understanding, interpreting of dreams, and showing of hard sentences, and dissolving of doubts, were found in the same Daniel, whom the king named Belteshazzar: now let Daniel be called, and he will show the interpretation.

Daniel 5:11-12

The understanding that comes from God is likened to light. The problems of life are darkness; so when that light comes, darkness has no choice but to give way. Psalm 112:4 says:

Unto the upright there ariseth light in the darkness...

There's a level of understanding you walk in that every hierarchy of darkness will have no choice but to give way when you are coming. Concerning Jesus, the Bible says in Luke 2:47:

And all that heard him were astonished at his understanding and answers.

Friend, there's a spirit called the Spirit of understanding. It is also known as the excellent spirit. It distinguished Daniel in the land of captivity. You are now in a free land, that same spirit will much more cheaply distinguish you, in the name of Jesus.

The Spirit of understanding is a gift from God.

> ***As for these four children, God gave them knowledge and skill in all learning and wisdom: and Daniel had understanding in all visions and dreams.***
>
> Daniel 1:17

"God gave them..." The Spirit of understanding comes from God. It was the chief reason for their outstanding accomplishments in the land of Babylon. He gave it to them then, and is still giving it today.

> ***Daniel answered and said, Blessed be the name of God for ever and ever: for wisdom and might are his:***
>
> ***And he changeth the times and the seasons: he removeth kings, and setteth up kings: he giveth wisdom unto the wise, and knowledge to them that know understanding:***
>
> ***He revealeth the deep and secret things: he knoweth what is in the darkness, and the light dwelleth with him.***
>
> ***I thank thee, and praise thee, O thou God of my fathers, who hast given me wisdom and might, and hast made known unto me now what we desired of thee: for thou hast now made known unto us the king's matter.***
>
> Daniel 2:20-23

That level of understanding is not possible, except by the finger of God! The Bible says that gift knows what is in the darkness. That's unusual insight! No wonder Daniel knew what was in darkness, and light dwelled with him.

Please note that there are two levels of understanding. One has to do with your spiritual understanding, while the other has to do with skillfulness in what God has planned for you from the beginning. Here are examples of both respectively:

> ***For this cause we also, since the day we heard it, do not cease to pray for you, and to desire that ye might be filled with the knowledge of his will in all wisdom and spiritual understanding.***
>
> Colossians 1:9

> ***And Moses said unto the children of Israel, See, the Lord hath called by name Bezaleel the son of Uri, the son of Hur, of the tribe of Judah;***
>
> ***And he hath filled him with the spirit of God, in wisdom, in understanding, and in knowledge, and in all manner of workmanship.***
>
> Exodus 35:30-31

I'd like you to lay hold on supernatural skill in handling whatever assignment God has placed in your hands. It will cause others to come and learn from you. Understanding guarantees the delivery of profit. Your result reveals the quality of the light you carry, and the quality of your life is a result of the level of light available to you.

Light is what is called understanding. It illuminates so as to reveal. There's a difference between knowledge and understanding. Knowledge is discovering what exists, while understanding is insight into it. Understanding tells you how to take delivery of what exists. May the Spirit of understanding distinguish you in this ongoing move of God.

The Spirit Of Counsel

This is the mother of visions and guidance. The Bible says:

> ***And thine ears shall hear a word behind thee, saying, This is the way, walk ye in it...***
>
> Isaiah 30:21

This is the mother of guidance; and it is one of the seven Spirits of the Lord. It guides your steps. The Spirit of counsel divinely orders your steps, so you will be free from all regrets.

God's guidance guarantees greatness. When you lay hold on His counsel, your destiny is secured. This is because when God tells you which way to go, that way must prosper. When He says to you, "Go!" no devil can stop you, and when He says, "Move!" no devil can push you down either. When God leads, it makes a leader of the led. If God leads you, you'll become a leader in that path He is leading you. That is the importance of the Spirit of counsel.

We are in the days of vision, so we need the operations of the Spirit of counsel more than ever before. The Spirit of counsel gives visions to men. It says to you, "This is the way, walk ye in it." It directs your path into the realms of excellence.

God's counsel guarantees the end (Isa. 46:9-10), as His counsel cannot be cancelled. When located and pursued, the end is secured. Also, when you invoke the release of the Spirit of counsel, all weariness, frustrations and regrets come to a final end — *"for (His) counsel it shall stand."* I have not taken any major step without the sound of the Spirit of counsel since 1976. That Spirit will guide you too from today!

Do you want to know how Jesus made it so great? He said:

> ***I can of mine own self do nothing: as I hear, I judge: and my judgment is just; because I seek not mine own will, but the will of the Father which hath sent me.***
>
> John 5:30

He was perfectly directed, so He made perfect impact everywhere He went. That was the mystery behind the exploits in His ministry. He had the release of the Spirit of counsel upon His life, and that made all the difference. No wonder the Psalmist said:

> ***The Lord is my shepherd; I shall not want.***
>
> ***He maketh me to lie down in green pastures: he leadeth me beside the still waters.***
>
> ***He restoreth my soul: he leadeth me in the paths of righteousness for his name's sake.***
>
> ***Yea, though I walk through the valley of the shadow of death, I will fear no evil: for thou art with me; thy rod and thy staff they comfort me.***
>
> ***Thou preparest a table before me in the presence of mine enemies: thou anointest my head with oil; my cup runneth over.***
>
> Psalm 23:1-5

What happens when the Lord is your Shepherd? Your enemies are rendered helpless, by virtue of the divine presence you carry. He will cause you to become an economic giant in the midst of economic crisis. You will also be bursting forth in sound health in the midst of an epidemic. His guidance is the mystery behind my stamina; that's what makes the difference in our ministry.

You need the Spirit of counsel to do exploits, because you need His guidance and visions to have manifestations. The Spirit of counsel is the force behind visions in life (Prov. 29:18). It offers guidance and direction, so that God's purpose for your life is not lost.

Jesus knew what He came for, but He still enjoyed the ministry of the Spirit of counsel throughout His time here on earth. When He was told that Lazarus was sick, the Bible says, *"He abode two days still in the place where he was"* (Jn. 11:6). Then on the third day, He said, *"Let us go..."* That was when the Spirit of counsel said to Him, "Move!" If He had moved earlier, Lazarus may not have woken up from the dead.

Friend, the Spirit of counsel will always lead you to the region of exploits. How we need that spirit today! King David always received counsel from God before he went forth to any battle; and every counsel from God produced results for him. When you are guided, you are guided into greatness and prominence. Let's lay hold on the ministry of the Spirit of counsel.

But how can we put this Spirit to work in our lives? By constantly inquiring of the Lord before you make any move. Before every move, always ask, "Spirit of God, this is what I'm thinking; but what are You saying?" And the Spirit of God will respond with specific instructions and direction. Like all things that has to do with the Spirit, do not let sin deafen your ears to hear His instructions, because He will surely speak.

It takes the ministry of the Holy Spirit to have meaning in the kingdom. Without the spirit of counsel, I would not be in ministry today, as the Spirit of counsel helps me improve on existing results. I command the same grace to come upon you, in the precious name of Jesus.

The Spirit Of Might

There is a Spirit of might. By this I mean that inner strength and tireless energy, the kind Jesus possessed. No vision can deliver results without strength, unique strength. You cannot walk in dominion if you are down today and up tomorrow. Paul knew this too well, hence he again prayed this prayer for the Ephesian Church:

> ***For this cause I bow my knees unto the Father of our Lord Jesus Christ,***
>
> ***Of whom the whole family in heaven and earth is named,***

That he would grant you, according to the riches of his glory, to be strengthened with might by his Spirit in the inner man.

Ephesians 3:14-16

Habakkuk 2:2 also says:

...Write the vision...that he may RUN that readeth it.

You need strength to run. God is going to deliver unusual strength to the end-time Church. Daniel 11:32 says it is those who do know their God that shall be strong and do exploits. You need strength to do exploits, and this strength can only be delivered to you by the Spirit of might.

Judges 15 tells us that when the Spirit came mightily upon Samson, he used the jawbone of an ass to slay one thousand Philistines. He uprooted the gate of a city (post and all), and carried it up the mountain! Samson was never down. As long as the Spirit of might was upon him, nobody could handle him. Receive that Spirit of might now, in Jesus' name!

Paul stayed in the deep (of the sea) for one whole night! At another time, he was stoned and left for dead. But no sooner had his "killers" turned their backs, than he jerked back to life! The man of war stood up and continued on his mission! Very strange strength – it was the Spirit of might at work. I see every weakness in your life die now, in Jesus name!

Every great accomplishment requires great strength to bring it to pass. Jesus taught for three days at a stretch; He was always on duty, *"about my Father's business"*, yet He never broke down. The Spirit of might was heavy upon His life.

There are many things your spirit wants to do, but your flesh is weak to do them. In Ephesians 3:16, we discover that the Spirit of God strengthens our inner man for exploits. Jesus said:

> ***I must work the works of him that sent me...***
>
> John 9:4

You need strength to do the work of the kingdom. If you do that work in the flesh, you will die cheaply, as there is no way you can pursue heavenly vision with natural strength.

The Root Of Might

Let me show you the source of the Spirit of might.

> ***The spirit of the Lord God is upon me...***
>
> ***To appoint unto them that mourn in Zion, to give unto them beauty for ashes, the OIL of JOY for mourning, the garment of praise for the spirit of***

> ***heaviness; that they might be called trees of righteousness, the planting of the Lord, that he might be glorified.***
>
> Isaiah 61:1,3

The Holy Spirit is sometimes known as *"The Oil of Joy."* The might of heaven is released upon you through avenues of joy. Show me a man that is never broken-hearted, and I will show you a man of unique strength. The oil of joy upon you automatically releases the Spirit of might. Look at Nehemiah 8:10

> ***...Neither be ye sorry; for the joy of the Lord is your strength.***

So the mystery of the Spirit of might is packaged in the oil of joy. This was what accounted for the unique strength in Jesus' ministry.

> ***Thou lovest righteousness, and hatest wickedness: therefore God, thy God, hath anointed thee with the oil of gladness above thy fellows.***
>
> Psalm 45:7

Jesus operated in the oil of gladness. It energizes the spirit-man; turning you into another man. I used to be weakling before that anointing came upon me. Now, I can do all things through Christ who strengthens me (Phil. 4:13).

The oil of gladness and joy is the secret behind the Spirit of might. Jesus had more of it than anybody else; no wonder He demonstrated more strength than anyone else. He was anointed *with the oil of gladness above His fellows.*

The Holy Ghost is the One who imparts joy unspeakable, that is full of glory, joy that cannot be explained in natural terms. Only the Holy Ghost can give you joy when things are not working. No matter what is happening around you, youare just on top! I see you come out of every sorrow of heart, in the name of Jesus! No matter what the situation is like, when you stick your life to the joy of the Holy Ghost, God makes some unique strength available to you, which will take you from the valley to your high places in life (Hab. 3:17-19).

The Bible says:

> ***A merry heart doeth good like a medicine: but a broken spirit drieth the bones.***
>
> Proverbs 17:22

Most sicknesses people suffer today are as a result of a broken heart. It is a broken heart that results in a broken body, as you are never broken outside until you are first broken inside. But when the inner-man is strengthened, the outer-man will be strong. That is why the Bible again says:

> ***The spirit of a man will sustain his infirmity; but a wounded spirit who can bear?***
>
> Proverbs 18:14

When your spirit is wounded, it takes your body along. So quit those depressive thoughts now. Every time your spirit is broken, it is an attempt of the devil to break your destiny. Stop him and connect yourself to the source of your help. Say to the Oil of Gladness, *"I want an encounter with You. Strengthen me with might in my inner-man."*

Joy is the secret of true strength; it is God's myth behind inner strength. In these days of exploits, you do not have a place without strength. Joel 2 gives a profile of the end-time army of exploit:

> ***The appearance of them is as the appearance of horses; and as horsemen, so shall they run.***
>
> ***Like the noise of chariots on the tops of mountains shall they leap, like the noise of a flame of fire that devoureth the stubble, as a strong people set in battle array.***
>
> ***They shall run like mighty men; they shall climb the wall like men of war; and they shall march every one on his ways, and they shall not break their ranks.***
>
> Joel 2:4-5,7

These are men of unique strength, and it's a function of the oil of gladness. Receive it today, in the name of Jesus!

The Spirit Of Knowledge

> ***But the Comforter, which is the Holy Ghost, whom the Father will send in my name, he shall teach you all things, and bring all things to your remembrance, whatsoever I have said unto you.***
>
> John 14:26

He will teach you all things — how to stay healthy, how to prosper, keep your home, raise children, make progress, have success, name it. Before I was married, the Holy Ghost taught me how to maintain a consistent and unbroken peace in my home. He also taught me how to maintain a financial flow in the covenant. He taught me how to stay alive and fulfill my days, that is why I am still alive today, in spite of all the attempts on my life. He equally taught me how to stay healthy, and it is almost 40 years since I was healed of tuberculosis. I'm still displaying health in the presence of my "enemies", and my health-cup "runneth over". All He taught me has stuck with me, and has made me great in life.

When the Holy Ghost teaches, it sticks to you, and makes you tick! If a man teaches, you may not fully understand, but when He teaches, the difference is clear! I do not mean verbal knowledge or intellectual exercise, but spiritual encounters with depth. The Bible says:

> ***And ye shall know the truth, and the truth shall make you free.***
>
> John 8:32

The Holy Spirit teaching you great depths from the Word of God is one of the fundamental truths of Christian triumph. It makes you a sweat less, triumphant Christian. He taught me how to succeed, and I have never feared failure since then. In fact, I wrote a book, *Success Buttons,* teaching people what keys to press to succeed in life. Everything I do succeeds, because He taught me. You can have a definite encounter with that same Spirit.

> ***That the God of our Lord Jesus Christ, the Father of glory, may give unto you the spirit of wisdom and revelation in the knowledge of him.***
>
> Ephesians 1:17

There is a Spirit called the Spirit of revelation. When you encounter the revelation knowledge of God on any issue, you become a man of exploits in that area. It is not enough to merely read or hear; you need to catch a revelation of what you are reading and hearing.

That is what makes the difference. The Psalmist said, *"God hath spoken once; twice have I heard..."* (Ps. 62:11). It is that second hearing that we call revelation and this Spirit is required to walk in dominion.

Revelation makes God's Word become personal to you — He turns the general Word into a personal word, which the charismatics call Rhema. Oh! God has spoken too many things to me that no man could have taught me. Note that when God teaches, it is an instruction; when you receive it, it becomes your manifestation.

Revelation is the ability to take delivery of instructions from God, as vision without instruction equals frustration. Knowing where you are going is good, but knowing how to get there is equally important, because you never get to your destination by just knowing where you are going. You also need to know how to get there.

> ***My people are destroyed for lack of knowledge...***
>
> Hosea 4:6

Not knowing what to do is the reason many in the Church are down and out today. But the Spirit of revelation cheaply commands the miraculous.

Please, note that the Spirit of knowledge is the same

one called the Spirit of revelation in Ephesians 1:17. This Spirit unfolds the mysteries of the kingdom of God.

> ***And he said unto them, Unto you it is given to know the mystery of the kingdom of God: but unto them that are without, all these things are done in parables.***
>
> Mark 4:11

Every kingdom mystery you grasp makes you gain mastery in that area. So, it is not enough to merely read. The Ethiopian eunuch was reading, but had no understanding. It took Philip asking him, *"Understandeth thou what thou readest?"* and expounding the scriptures to him for him to grasp what he was reading (Acts 8:30-35). It is the Spirit of revelation that reveals the mysteries of the kingdom to us.

The Spirit of knowledge destroys ignorance. It is my belief that you are not suffering because there is a great devil somewhere, but rather because of your great ignorance. But when the Spirit of revelation takes over in your life, just one scripture you read will give you multiple interpretations, until your manifestation is delivered to you. You know that when light challenges darkness, darkness gives way immediately.

I knew I would never be poor long ago, not because God appeared to me in a dream, but because I saw it from His Word, the Bible. I knew the day I saw it; it was so real. When God reveals a thing to you, you can't be confused about it. Revelation is the bedrock for every revolution in the kingdom. No wonder apostle Paul said:

> ***Now we have received, not the spirit of the world, but the spirit which is of God; that we might know the things that are freely given to us of God.***
>
> 1 Corinthians 2:12

So that Spirit delivers to us the things that are freely given to us of God, and teaches us how to lay hold on them. There are things freely given to you, which you have not been able to receive, because they have not yet been revealed to you. You do not have to be sick for instance, let alone be hospitalised. You do not have to be poor. It is your ignorance of abundance that has kept you in lack. You do not have to suffer crisis in your home either. Your ignorance of God's instructions for a peaceful home is what is causing hardship and crisis for you. I took instructions on how to run the ministry, how to manage my home, how to develop an ever-growing ministry, and how to grow a big church from the Bible!

That Book is full of instructions. But those who miss the instructions it contains suffer devastations and destructions. Only the Holy Ghost delivers them to people, so you must accept His help right now, as He is willing to teach you.

Do you know that the men who the Bible records as turning the world upside down were ignorant and unlearned men? They didn't go to any school, as most of them were fishermen. But they were carriers of the Spirit of knowledge and revelation (Acts 4:13, 17:6)! The wisdom of the Holy Ghost was what gave them all that unusual insight they so boldly declared. Such wisdom is too high for the ordinary mind, so it's time to go to the "School of the Spirit".

The Spirit of revelation also puts you in charge, giving you dominion.

> ***They shall not hurt nor destroy in all my holy mountain: for the earth shall be full of the knowledge of the Lord, as the waters cover the sea.***
>
> Isaiah 11:9

The end-time Church is destined to display strange authority, because of the knowledge of the Lord that is operating within her.

This Spirit also shows you a better way of doing things. Until you destroy tradition, you never gain access to the truth. There is a better way to do what you are doing now, that will take you to higher heights. The Spirit of knowledge will show it to you.

Paul said in 1 Corinthians 3:10, *"I have laid the foundation, and another buildeth thereon."* So we have the power to build on where they stopped. I never saw where Paul breathe into someone, but I caught something brighter than he did — that God breathe into clay, and it became a living being (Gen. 2:7). Operating in this revelation, I met a woman who was suffering from AIDS, in Kampala, Uganda, and I said to her, "Open your mouth!" She did, and I breathe into her mouth and cursed AIDS. I told the people around, "Watch it, she's alive!"

Again, there was this little girl who had not had a bowel movement for five days, and her father was in tears, because her stomach was already protruding. Again, I breathe into her mouth, and few minutes later, she emptied the whole junk inside her into the toilet. Something penetrated the regions of darkness and shattered it!

A pregnant woman met me and was crying. Hospital reports said her baby was breech, and she was due for delivery and was full of agitation. I asked her, "When do you want to have your baby?" And she replied,

"I'm already due." I told her to open her mouth, I breathe into her, instructing her to, "Go and have your baby now!" They did not get home from church before labour started! They had to drive into the nearest hospital. By the time her husband returned with the baby's things, he heard the cry of their newborn baby!

Revelation is developing life equations from scriptures, for outstanding solutions. It is knowing what God is saying, and putting them together in order to punish the devil and give him a technical knockout!

But note that it is not for natural men. The Bible says:

> ***But the natural man receiveth not the things of the Spirit of God: for they are foolishness unto him: neither can he know them, because they are spiritually discerned.***
>
> 1 Corinthians 2:14

You can be intellectually sound and yet be a spiritual dummy. This is because it is only the Spirit of God that knows the things of God. Therefore, only He can show it to you (1 Cor. 2:10). The Bible says it is when you know the truth that you will be free. So how much of the things of God the Spirit of God teaches you is what determines how free you will be.

Also, please note that no one who enjoys sin can ever have access into the mysteries of the kingdom of God, because they are in parables to them that are without (Mk. 4:11). They will sound as mere stories to those who wallow in sin. So it is important that you stay clean, so that the access remains open to you.

The Spirit Of The Fear Of The Lord

There is something that gives birth to unprecedented exploits; it is called the fear of the Lord. For instance, Joseph, a man discreet and wise, who through his wisdom saved Egypt in the time of famine, said concerning himself, *"For I fear God"* (Gen. 42:18). Job was described as the greatest of all men of the East. Satan acknowledged him as possessing one outstanding quality — the fear of the Lord! *"Doth Job fear God for nought?"* Satan asked (Job 1:9).

Looking at all seven Spirits of God listed in Isaiah 11:2, we observe that the root of this latter rain is the fear of the Lord. It is at the bottom rung of the ladder. And just as every ladder is climbed from the bottom, you climb into the fullness of the seven Spirits from the Spirit of the fear of the Lord. The spirit of the fear of the Lord is what gives birth to the spirit of knowledge.

The fear of the Lord is the beginning of knowledge...

Proverbs 1:7

Knowledge then brings you into might, which is inner strength.

...A man of knowledge increaseth strength.

Proverbs 24:5

From might you graduate to counsel. From counsel to understanding, then to wisdom, which culminates in manifestations of power.

Please understand this: the world will not fear you until your fear of God is in place. Satan will not fear you until your fear of God is established. Sickness will not fear you until your fear of God is in place. Neither will failure fear you, until your fear of God is intact. So, it is your fear of God that gives you your place on the earth.

And unto man he said, Behold, the fear of the Lord, that is wisdom...

Job 28:28

When the fear of the Lord is at work in you, you will overturn the mountains by the roots (Job 28:9-11). That is, you will convert obstacles to miracles.

You will cut out rivers among the rocks. That is, you will flourish, in spite of the hardship on the earth. You will also be able to stop every form of wickedness around you. Destruction and death will fear you too (vs. 22).

God's presence is guaranteed when the fear of the Lord is in place in your life. The thrice-Holy God demands holiness from you. If you don't let Him have it, neither will you have Him! God demands our holiness for us to enjoy His presence. We cannot have His presence until we give Him what it takes.

I'd like you to understand that nothing is more valuable than divine presence in your Christian adventure. That is your greatest asset. And the fear of the Lord is the price to pay for it. Without His presence your place on earth will be lost, and your hope of getting to heaven will be uncertain.

The Spirit of the fear of the Lord is what Apostle Paul refers to as the *"Spirit of holiness"* in Romans 1:3-4:

> ***Concerning his Son Jesus Christ our Lord, which was made of the seed of David according to the flesh;***
>
> ***And declared to be the Son of God with power, according to the spirit of holiness, by the resurrection from the dead.***

Jesus was declared to be the Son of God with power because the spirit of holiness was at work in Him. He was tempted at all points, yet was without sin, so He qualified to be anointed without measure. Jesus knew no sin, no wonder He knew no defeat. He was in touch with heaven. Since He walked in purity, the Father always responded to Him. In fact, Jesus was dedicated to doing only the things that pleased God.

> ***And he that sent me is with me: the Father hath not left me alone; for I do always those things that please him.***
>
> John 8:29

If God is holy, you cannot walk with Him except you are holy. The Bible asked in Psalm 24:3-4:

> ***Who shall ascend into the hill of the Lord? or who shall stand in his holy place?***
>
> ***He that hath clean hands, and a pure heart; who hath not lifted up his soul unto vanity, nor sworn deceitfully.***

When you walk with God, you are guaranteed automatic exploits. His presence commands exploits — the sea gives way to Him, and Jordan is driven back for Him. The mountains skip like rams before Him (Ps. 114). But sin repels God's presence. So, when sin disappears, His presence is made manifest, and exploits are inevitable. The barrier between man and the flow of the Spirit of the fear of the Lord is sin. Until the sin barrier is broken down, man's separation from God remains.

When you become free from sin, you become a friend of God and you have access to all things that the Father has shown Jesus. When this happens, friend, you begin to operate at the level Jesus operated, and you begin to do the type of exploits He did, and even greater as He promised.

The seven Spirits of God gave Jesus His throne; they will give you yours also! When the former rain came, He said, *"You shall be endued with power from on high."* But He promised to give us both the former and the latter rain in the first month. So in our time, we are going to experience the six other Spirits in practical manifestation — the Spirit of wisdom, the Spirit of understanding, the Spirit of counsel, the Spirit of might, the Spirit of knowledge, and the Spirit of the fear of the Lord.

When the seven Spirits of God are at work in you, your rest shall be glorious. You will become more than a conqueror in the conflicts of life, and you will walk on in dominion.

Now pray this prayer with me:

"Lord, let all Your waves and billows come over me! I want to have an encounter with the seven Spirits of God."

The Love Dimension

In addition to possessing the seven Spirits of God, which is working mightily in these last days to bring the Church to its' prophetic and colourful stature, I would like to point out the place of one other important force by which the Holy Spirit will be distinguishing us these last days. It is an attribute of the Spirit of the fear of the Lord. It is the love dimension. John 14:21 says:

> ***He that hath my commandments, and keepeth them, he it is that loveth me: and he that loveth me shall be loved of my Father, and I will love him, and will manifest myself to him.***

Paul said in 2 Timothy 1:7:

> ***For God hath not given us the spirit of fear; but of power, and of love, and of a sound mind.***

There is such thing as the Spirit of love. It is that spirit that gets you addicted to God; it is what makes you a man after God's own heart. The spirit of love begins with affection, graduates to devotion, and then matures into addiction. I want you to ask to be possessed by this Spirit of love.

I am one of very many "God-addicts" on the earth today. I'm addicted! I celebrate Jesus as my focus and my reason for living. As a result, I noted in my Bible: "My soul, keep blowing hotter and hotter, until youare face to face with the Master. I shall keep blowing hot, no matter what others are blowing!"

You too need to say this prayer:

"Lord, possess me with Your Spirit of love. Get me addicted to You the remaining days of my life. Keep me on key with You, so I can be free from the spirit of the world."

When you are possessed with the Spirit of love, every other thing in the world naturally loses value to you, and yet you keep increasing in value. You cannot be addicted to God and not be added to. Friend, with the Spirit of love at work in you, you will gain command over the things that want to compete with God in your life. That way, you will never miss your manifestation in life, and you'll win everywhere - at home, at work, on the street, anywhere!

When you are possessed with the Spirit of love, you will stay above board, and the things of this world will be unable to distract you. And as you are possessed with His love, He makes you a possessor on the earth, because no one is possessed of God who does not possess the earth.

Love never dies! David loved God so much that even God described him as a man after His heart. In Jerusalem a few years back, they celebrated the 3,000th year that David declared Jerusalem the City of David. You mean after 3,000 years, they have not forgotten the man? Yes! Because love never dies! You too will possess your own inheritance on this earth!

David's love for God was what took him to the throne. Love drove him to challenge and fight Goliath, and love brought him the victory. Love is greater than faith; for there are three forces — faith, hope and love; but the greatest of these is love (1 Cor. 13:13)!

If by taking the shield of faith you can quench all the fiery darts of the devil, then by walking in love, you will quench the devil himself! Why? God's Word says in 1 John 4:16:

> ***And we have known and believed ...(that) he that dwelleth in love dwelleth in God, and God in him.***

That means the love of God makes you become a

partaker of God. The nature of God begins to flow inside you, and Satan cannot handle that! That is an automatic route to dominion! When Jesus came here, demons were screaming. Why? God was too much inside Him! In fact, He said, *"He that has seen me, has seen the Father."* And the demons screamed, *"Have you come to destroy us before the time?"*

First John 4:17 tells us:

> ***Herein is our love made perfect, that we may have boldness in the day of judgment: because as he is, so are we in this world.***

So when our love is perfected, we bodily represent His personality, giving no room for the devil. That was the realm Jesus operated in; and as He is, so are we now in this world. When our love is perfected, we fully partake of His divine nature, which makes it easy for us to exercise dominion on the earth.

Oh, Lord, rain Your rain of love upon my heart, anoint me afresh with the Spirit of love! I want my heaven to stay open, so Lord anoint me with the Spirit of love. I want to stay addicted to You and to Your kingdom upon the earth.

The Place Of Impartation

Impartation is another covenant way of walking in dominion. This is because through it, you are able to stand on the shoulders of those who have gone ahead of you, and enjoy their victories. You do not have to make the mistakes they made; you only share in their successes.

Nothing is more authentic than that which comes direct from source. Every letter in the Bible is gathered by the Spirit (Isa. 34:16), so every time the Word is going forth, the Spirit is also going forth, seeking entrance into people. The Spirit of God gathered the whole Bible, from Genesis to Revelation.

Knowing this first, that no prophecy of the scripture is of any private interpretation.

> ***For the prophecy came not in old time by the will of man: but holy men of God spake as they were moved by the Holy Ghost.***
>
> 2 Peter 1:20-21

Therefore, when the Word is being spoken, you are not just encountering insights; you are also encountering the impartation of the Spirit that gathered it. Do not make light anymore the time you spend listening to anointed teachers and preachers of the Word. And when you listen and hear, do not only expect to receive insight; expect and prepare your heart to encounter the power of God as well.

The spoken word of God comes to us in many forms - audio and videotapes, television, radio, etc., and many have encountered power through them. People have encountered the baptism of fresh oil as they listened to the spoken Word. When you present your heart as a tablet, you don't only receive insight, but you also receive an impartation that will enable the insight to produce.

In 1987, I watched a videotape based on a message from Isaiah 53:1: "Who hath believed our report? and to whom is the arm of the Lord revealed?" My heart and eyes were glued to the programme. As I watched and listened to that crusade message, the power of God hit me so hard that I was in tears. I was there alone in the house. I went to bed in that state.

There was such a quickening in me, that I rose up early, went to the living room, and cried out, "God, show me the secret!" Then I heard a man walk into the room and place His hand on my back, and some waves went down my spine. I burst into tears.

I stood up to preach in church the following Sunday. I said, "Let's welcome ourselves with this scripture..." and we opened to Psalm 110. But before I could finish reading it, the power of God came down! There was no further preaching; instead, there were all manner of healings! What happened that day in church was what gave rise to the programme, "Pentecost Flames", which was the stirring and devil–destroying invasion of Kaduna State, a city in northern Nigeria.

I was imparted with strange power from watching that tape, which launched our ministry into another phase. There is power in Word encounter! Until you are a Word–lover you do not experience power. The genuine source of power is the Word. Acts 10:44 records that, *"While Peter yet spake these words, the Holy Ghost fell on all them which heard the word."* An impartation takes place as words are being spoken. An impartation also takes place as prophetic utterances are made. No wonder Prophet Ezekiel said:

> ***And the spirit entered into me when he spake unto me...***
>
> Ezekiel 2:2

As you hear anointed words, do not only expect to get insight, but expect to encounter impartation as well.

In 1986, I attended a meeting in Tulsa, Oklahoma, where the late Reverend Kenneth E. Hagin was ministering. I was seated afar off in the gallery. But as he was speaking, I saw his face transfigured into that of a little baby (I don't know how many people saw what I saw). But I had an encounter there and then! My heart exploded, and I began to sob openly. The

Spirit entered into me and changed the entire course of my ministry!

Before then, I used to jump all over the place, sweating as I preached. But from that day that the Spirit entered into me, the serenity of Kenneth Hagin's style of ministration was imparted to me.

Once I was watching Archbishop Benson Idahosa teach on a videotape, and for the first time in my life, an unseen guest walked up to me. His footsteps were audible to me. And as he put his hands on my back, something went through me. That was when the anointing for miracles was released upon me. Ever since then, I see disease as fake and see those who sympathize with it as ignorant. I see that you can be well if it is your desire to be well.

In 1979, I heard an audio message preached by A. A. Allen (about ten years before he went to be with the Lord), in which he spoke some powerful things that have become one of the pillars of my insights in God today. The message was titled, *"The Lord killeth and He maketh alive!"* All the feminine nature in me died after listening to that message! My heart received an inoculation of confidence and boldness.

After then, I could dare a lion without any shaking in my heart. A. A. Allen had gone to be with the Lord when I heard that message, but that message became my greatest treasure. I guarded it jealously.

Everybody is conversant with the prayer dimension of seeking the power of God, but this is another dimension that makes it very outstanding and glorious. When you are exposed to anointed teachings, you contact power that causes you to walk in dominion. The more exposed you are to anointed words at seminars, conventions or church services, the more access you have to the power of God.

One can then understand what Peter meant in Acts 6:2,4, when he said:

> ***...It is not reason that we should leave the word of God, and serve tables...***
>
> ***But we will give ourselves continually to prayer, and to the ministry of the word.***

These two operations — prayer and ministry of the Word will keep us fresh and powerful for exploits.

Anointed Books

Anointed books are divine expositions on the Bible,

which help to break it down to a point where you can easily understand what is being said. Anointed books help to fill you with more light.

I read a book titled, *"The Apostle of Faith"* in 1979. It was about the great man of God, Smith Wigglesworth. I caught a very powerful insight from that book, which filled my spirit-man with a violent anger against the devil. As I read the testimony of how Smith Wigglesworth treated the devil (when he saw him sitting on a rocking chair in his living room), the Spirit entered me, and I saw the nothingness of the devil. Since then, I treat the devil as though he were nothing. In fact, I wrote a book titled, *"Satan Get Lost!"*

I also read a book in 1974, titled, *"Like a Mighty Wind"*, by Merl and Lona Tari. That book gave me an appetite for the miraculous. My stomach would no longer be satisfied with ordinary Christianity. I saw God in the wilderness of Indonesia, where ordinary men like me were re-enacting the Acts of the Apostles! I stored that book on my inside, as I read it over and over again. I kept saying to myself,

"This is true Christianity! This is the one Jesus brought", not the type I was in then, which was what men brought by their own creed.

Open your heart whenever you are reading anointed books, and whatever is missing in your life will be supplied. This is because where you are is a function of what you discover. You must make more discoveries to go beyond where you are now.

Contact With The Anointed

Contact with the anointed (anointed men and women), especially when you have a sense of value for it, automatically transmits power to you. Many have taken this lightly, but I tell you, it is scriptural.

> ***And Joshua the son of Nun was full of the spirit of wisdom; for Moses had laid his hands upon him...***
>
> Deuteronomy 34:9

The laying-on of the hands of the anointed servant of God, Moses, released wisdom on Joshua. Paul admonished Timothy in 2 Timothy 1:6 to:

> ***...Stir up the gift of God, which is in thee by the putting on of my hands.***

Your sense of value when you come in contact with

the anointed of God determines the flow of virtue to you. The people from Nazareth, the place where Jesus grew up, saw Him as merely the son of Joseph the carpenter, so nothing went out from Him to them. The Bible records that Jesus could not do mighty works there, because of their unbelief (Mk. 6:1-6). But the woman with the issue of blood knew Him as the Messiah, healer and deliverer, so she was determined to receive her miracle. She had the correct sense of value, so she was healed when she touched the hem of Jesus' garment.

I was in a place in the United States of America, and was told that Kenneth Copeland had once slept in the same room. I looked up to heaven and said, "God, You know how much I love Copeland's ministry, how much I appreciate Your hand upon his life. You know how much he has affected our world for You, and how much he has proved the devil wrong in demonstrating that You bless those You have called. Lord, as I go to sleep on this bed tonight, let what works in Copeland begin to work in me." That contact turned my financial status around, all because I had the correct sense to recognise my superior. God has lifted Kenneth Copeland, and I was taking advantage of an opportunity to climb upon his shoulders.

I saw a vision that night. In that vision, I saw an amputated hand, and worms coming out from the stump of the hand. It had rejected all treatment. But right in that same vision, I said, "In the name of Jesus!" and before my eyes, a brand new hand grew out! In that same vision, God spoke to me saying, "I have brought you into the creative realm of your ministry." That was a few years ago, and God has stayed true to His Word.

Friend, just a handshake with the anointed of God can change your stagnant life, and destroy that disease in your body. A look into the eyes of the anointed can mean the beginning of an entirely new era in your life, depending on your sense of value. Just like Copeland has no problem with means, I also have no problem with means. I don't sell anything; I'm not in any business at all in this world. I'm simply trading the covenant, and with open eyes, looking for where the higher anointing is, to tap into it.

Let's imbibe a new sense of value. Timothy's greatness came by the laying-on of the hands of Paul. Whether the anointed person is a man or woman is irrelevant, for there's neither male nor female, Jew nor Greek (Rom. 10:12). It was a woman that led me to Christ, and it was also a woman that taught me the way into abundance, through her book. So, I don't care who it is, as long as I sense the power of God on the person, I just open my heart to receive. Any encounter with the anointed means a lot to your destiny, so let's go for it.

In the book of Acts of the Apostles, even the shadow of Peter was healing the sick. Aprons and handkerchiefs were being taken from Paul's body to heal the sick and deliver the oppressed. Devils were being cast out.

As you come in contact with anointed men and women, open your heart. Isaac Newton said, "If I've seen any further, it's by standing on the shoulders of those who have gone before me." Pride is a destroyer! There is no self-made man. Every man of worth is a man of references. Your papers are usually not acknowledged (for employment, contracts, or whatever) until you have adequate references. Don't strive to be self-made; otherwise, you will be self-destroyed!

Embrace the anointed of God from afar. Desire the hand of God upon them, and very soon you will see the same anointing they carry flowing through to you. The entire ministry of Elisha was a product of Elijah's ministry, and he was never ashamed of it. When he came face-to-face with river Jordan in 2 Kings 2:13-14, he said, "Where is the Lord God of Elijah?" as he struck the river with the mantle that had fallen from Elijah.

Anyone you are ashamed of cannot be a source of power for you. But any vessel you genuinely embrace, if he is anointed of God, the anointing upon him will flow across to you. Remember that what went into Timothy was not the gift of Paul, but the gift of God, transmitted via the hands of Paul. So, whether you encounter the anointing via the Word, by prayer, or whether it is through contact with anointed people or by laying-on of hands, it is the same power of

God. They all release the fresh anointing, stirring up the gift of God inside you.

Every anointed vessel is a reservoir of power, from where everyone goes to draw according to his thirst. It, therefore, matters how you appreciate contact with the anointed. Please take advantage of this gift from God; it is for your own good.

Fear Not!

The wicked flee when no man pursueth: but the righteous are bold as a lion.

Proverbs 28:1

You have to be fearless in order to truly walk in dominion. This is because fear deflates power. God has deposited in you all that it takes to walk in dominion, as we have discussed in the preceding chapters. It will, therefore, be an insult on redemption for you to still walk with your head bowed down, rather than walk tall and fearless like the victor and conqueror that you are.Consider this assurance from the Lord. I pray it will further boost your confidence in Him.

> ***When thou goest out to battle against thine enemies, and seest horses, and chariots, and a people more than thou, be not afraid of them: for the Lord thy God is with thee, which brought thee up out of the land of Egypt.***
>
> ***And it shall be, when ye are come nigh unto the battle, that the priest shall approach and speak unto the people.***
>
> ***And shall say unto them, Hear, O Israel, ye approach this day unto battle against your enemies: let not your hearts faint, fear not, and do not tremble, neither be ye terrified because of them;***
>
> ***For the Lord your God is he that goeth with you, to fight for you against your enemies, to save you.***
>
> Deuteronomy 20:1-4

Be assured of this fact, that *"the Lord your God is he that goeth with you, to fight for you against your enemies."* Not only that, He is with you to save you. Know for a surety that the verdict of the battle has been given in your favour. Heaven has declared you the victor in every battle you are confronted with. This should cause you to walk tall.

Fear is a snare; it brings men into bondage. You will not become an overcomer until you overcome it. Fear is a principal hurdle you must overcome before you can become a winner in life. When you see horses and chariots all around you, and the people are perhaps greater in number than you are, God says to you, *"Be not afraid, for I am with thee."*

Shortly before He left this earth, Jesus said to us:

> ***...Lo, I am with you alway, even to the end of the world.***
>
> Matthew 28:20

Paul also said in Romans 8:31, *"If God be for us, who can be against us?"* And the Psalmist said, *"Though I walk through the valley of the shadow of death, I shall fear no evil: for thou art with me"* (Ps. 23:4). God is, therefore, saying to you today, "Stand up and face your challenges. I am going to fight for you and save you."

Fear will always bring defeat your way. But we are in the day of His power, a time for you to walk in dominion and not fear. You already have an anointing for battle, that will make you unmovable as mount Zion.

> ***They that trust in the Lord shall be as mount Zion, which cannot be removed, but abideth for ever.***
>
> ***As the mountains are round about Jerusalem, so***

> ***the Lord is round about his people from henceforth even for ever.***
>
> ***For the rod of the wicked shall not rest upon the lot of the righteous; lest the righteous put forth their hands unto iniquity.***
>
> Psalm 125:1-3

You must be able to say like Paul, *"But none of these things move me."* All you need is to be steadfast. The Bible tells us to *"Stand fast therefore in the liberty wherewith Christ hath made us free"* (Gal. 5:1). God is committed to ensuring that no rod of the wicked rests upon you and all that concerns you. But the fearful have no future in any battle. Rise up, therefore, to the challenge around you. We are fighting a battle that has already been won; and the Captain of hosts, the Lord, the Man of war, is He that fights for us!

Another way to overcome fear is to be always conscious of the fact that the Lord your God is with you always. The devil has appointed giants to scare you away from every Canaan appointed for you. But you and I are creatures of destiny, so we have to be bold as a lion and confront all the giants on the way to our Canaan. Also know that heaven will rise up to destroy any giant that attempts to stand in your way. Don't let anybody stop you from reaching your

Canaan.

Without a heart you cannot make a mark. In warfare, every fearful person is disqualified. God is arming His Church, and we are privileged to be in the forefront, fully armed. So, get on the road, for this is your hour of manifestation; it's time to dare the devil. He will surely surrender to you.

Unparalleled confidence is what makes a conqueror. The inner strength of conquerors is unbeatable and within you already, for we are told that we are more than conquerors. You must become power-conscious, otherwise the wicked forces on this earth won't let you live.

Jesus said in Mark 11:23:

> ***For verily I say unto you, That whosoever shall say unto this mountain, Be thou removed, and be thou cast into the sea; and shall not doubt in his heart, but shall believe that those things which he saith shall come to pass; he shall have whatsoever he saith.***

It is time to tell the mountains on your way to get lost. They are not part of your inheritance. Business frustrations and failure are not part of your inheritance. The power to disarm your enemy is in your hand, so no Pharaoh should be able to torment you any longer. Just as Pharaoh was helpless before Moses, so every opposition has become helpless before you, in Jesus' name! From now on, at your appearance, every closed gate shall be lifted up, and every Red Sea shall give way! Every mountain shall skip like rams at your appearance, and every valley shall be filled!

The time for you to wallow in signs and wonders has come. The time has come for everything that hitherto made you hide your face in the society and in the neighbourhood to be swallowed up. Your slavery has come to an end, in Jesus precious name!

Walk in dominion, be bold as a lion, like the sister in this testimony:

"I'm a senior nursing sister. There was a woman in labour yesterday, who had been in labour since the night before. I did not go into the Labour Room immediately I got to work yesterday, because I was late to work. But later in the afternoon, when I was with the Medical Director, one of the doctors came in to say, 'Sir, I have a very difficult labour. That woman is likely to go for a Caesarean Section. She had her first baby like that as well.'

The woman had what we call CPD (Chephalo Pelvic Disproportion). The baby looked big and so could not come out. Ideally, for someone who had had a baby before, her rate of contraction and dilation should be faster. But as at 12 noon yesterday morning, she was still four centimeters dilated. The doctors were worried and had began preparing her for an operation.

I was downstairs monitoring the antenatal patients when I heard a voice say, 'Leave whatever you are doing, and go to the Labour Room.' I was almost disobeying the voice, because a nurse was already assigned to her. But the voice insisted, so I obeyed. When I got to the Labour Room and saw the woman, I discovered that she was a fellow Winner. I asked, 'What happened to you?' She said, 'I've been in labour since.' I said, 'What did you do? Where is your anointing oil?' She said it was in her bag outside. I then asked her, 'How can you leave your anointing oil in the bag outside?'

I went outside to collect it, and applied it on her abdomen and on the passage through which the baby would come. I said, 'The Bishop said no knife shall cut our bodies again. So, since you're a Winner, although you had your first baby by C.S., this one is going to come out through normal birth.'

The woman again said, 'Fellow Winner, I have the blood of sprinkling in my bag outside.' I went and collected it. The Spirit of the Lord instructed me to sprinkle the Labour Room with the blood, and I obeyed. The Spirit of the Lord said I shouldn't pray, so I started singing praises. The first song that came to my mind was the Yoruba song that says we have a Father as a defence. I gave her a capful of the blood of Jesus and struck her with my mantle seven times, calling on the Lord God of Bishop Oyedepo.

I said, 'Lord, this is 2.30 P.M., I'm closing from work at 3.30 P.M. I want this baby out by then, because I must see this baby before I leave for home.' To the glory of God, the woman put to bed at exactly five minutes to three o'clock! But the baby came out limp. As medical people, they wanted to rush oxygen and so on, but I told them to leave the baby alone. I again got hold of the blood of Jesus, and sprinkled it on the baby. For someone that had refused to cry, he cried as though someone just gave him a whack on the back!"

Ajayi, M.D. (Mrs.)

This sister knew who she was and what she carried, so was bold to step in and take charge. She was also not afraid to use her dominion weapons. You too must arise and take charge. It's the season for the manifestations of the sons of God, the time to chase every wicked force into hiding. It's your responsibility to do it, because God has put you in charge.

Arise, and walk in dominion!

Books by Dr. David O. Oyedepo

- Signs & Wonders Today
- Exploits In Ministry
- Winning The War Against Poverty
- Walking In Dominion
- Possessing Your Possession
- The Wisdom That Works
- Exploits Of Faith
- Anointing For Exploits
- Understanding The Power Of Praise
- Walking In Newness Of Life
- Maximise Destiny
- Commanding The Supernatural
- Winning Invisible Battles
- Success Systems
- Understanding Financial Prosperity
- Success Strategies
- Understanding Your Covenant Right
- Operating In The Supernatural
- Miracle Meal
- Exploring the Riches of Redemption
- Towards Excellence In Life & Ministry
- Anointing For Breakthrough
- Releasing The Supernatural
- Excellency Of Wisdom
- Breaking Financial Hardship
- The Release Of Power
- Walking In The Miraculous

- Satan Get Lost!
- The Winning Wisdom
- Walking In Wisdom
- The Healing Balm
- Emergence Of The Glorious Church
- Breaking The Curses Of Life
- Overcoming Forces Of Wickedness
- You Shall Not Be Barren!
- Exploring The Secrets Of Success

Winning Prayer

- Understanding The Anointing
- Fulfilling Your Days
- Riding On Prophetic Wings
- Towards Mental Exploits
- Making Maximum Impact
- Understanding Vision
- Understanding Divine Direction
- Keys To Divine Health
- The Force Of Freedom
- Born To Win

MINI BOOKS

- All You Need To Have All Your needs Met
- The Blood Triumph
- Conquering Controlling Powers
- The Mystery Of Anointing Oil
- Put Your Angels To Work
- Covenant Wealth
- Hidden Covenant Of Blessings
- The Law Of Faith
- Keys To Answered Prayer
- Miracle Seed
- The Path Of The Eagles

ABOUT THE AUTHOR

For more than two decades, Dr. David O. Oyedepo, has been part of the current charismatic renaissance sweeping through the African continent. His faith-based teachings have transformed millions of lives.

Called with a specific mandate to liberate mankind from all oppressions of the devil, Dr. Oyedepo is the President of Living Faith Church Worldwide Inc. With a network of churches all over Nigeria and most nations of Africa.

He is also the Senior Pastor of the 50,000 capacity - Faith Tabernacle, Canaan Land, Ota, a suburb of Lagos, Nigeria reputed to be the largest church auditorium in the world.

As an educationist, his mission currently pioneers the establishment of educational institutions at all levels in Nigeria, including the recently established Covenant University, where he serves as the Chancellor.

He has written over 50 titles of inspirational and educative texts covering various aspects of life.

He is married to Faith, and their marriage is blessed with children.

INSIDE VIEW OF
Faith Tabernacle
OUTSIDE VIEW OF FAITH TABERNACLE
CHURCH MASS TRANSIT— Over 250 buses commuting the worshippers to Church from all nook and crannies of Lagos & environs
Dr. David Oyedepo is the founding president of the Living Faith Church Worldwide Inc. And senior pastor of the Faith Tabernacle, a 50,000 capacity sanctuary located in Canaan Land, Ota, a suburb of Lagos Nigeria.
The construction of this gigantic architectural masterpiece was completed within twelve months and dedicated on September 18, 1999. Built totally debt free and without any foreign inputs! To God alone be all the glory.
Today, Faith Tabernacle stands as the home of signs and wonders for men and women all over the world who keep
Visit our website for more information: www.davidoyedepoministries.org

An aerial view of section of CU Campus

College of Business & Social Sciences

More Facilities@ Covenant University

College of Science & Technology

University Library (Centre For Learning Resources)

Students Hall Of Residence

Students Hall Of Residence

0 Seat Students Chapel

Senior Staff Residential Quarters